CH00470963

YOUR CОMPLETE CAPRICORN 2024 PERSONAL HOROSCOPE

Monthly Astrological Prediction Forecast Readings of Every Zodiac Astrology Sun Star Signs- Love, Romance, Money, Finances, Career, Health, Travel, Spirituality.

Iris Quinn

Alpha Zuriel Publishing

Your Complete Capricorn 2024 Personal Horoscope/ Iris Quinn. -- 1st ed.

"In the dance of the planets, we find the rhythms of life. Astrology reminds us that we are all connected to the greater universe, and our actions have ripple effects throughout the cosmos."
— IRIS QUINN

CONTENTS

CHAPTER ONE

CAPRICORN PROFILE

- Constellation: Capricorn
- Zodiac symbol: Goat
- Date: December 22 - January 19
- Element: Earth
- Ruling Planet: Saturn
- Career Planet: Saturn
- Love Planet: Venus
- Money Planet: Saturn
- Planet of Fun, Entertainment, Creativity, and Speculations: Venus
- Planet of Health and Work: Moon
- Planet of Home and Family Life: Saturn
- Planet of Spirituality: Mars
- Planet of Travel, Education, Religion, and Philosophy: Jupiter

Colors:
• Colors: Dark Green, Brown

- Colors that promote love, romance, and social harmony: Pink, Pale Yellow
- Color that promotes earning power: Black

Gem: Garnet
Metals: Lead, Silver
Scent: Musk
Birthstone: Garnet

Qualities:
• Quality: Cardinal (represents activity)
• Quality most needed for balance: Flexibility

Strongest Virtues:
• Responsibility
• Discipline
• Ambition
• Loyalty
• Practicality

Deepest Need: Stability

Characteristics to Avoid:
• Rigidity
• Pessimism
• Materialism
• Stubbornness

Signs of Greatest Overall Compatibility:
• Taurus
• Virgo

Signs of Greatest Overall Incompatibility:
• Aries
• Libra
• Cancer

- Sign Most Supportive for Career Advancement: Capricorn
- Sign Most Supportive for Emotional Well-being: Taurus
- Sign Most Supportive Financially: Taurus
- Sign Best for Marriage and/or Partnerships: Cancer
- Sign Most Supportive for Creative Projects: Virgo
- Best Sign to Have Fun With: Leo

Signs Most Supportive in Spiritual Matters:
• Pisces
• Taurus

Best Day of the Week: Saturday

CAPRICORN TRAITS

- Adventurous nature coupled with a desire for freedom and exploration.
- Optimistic outlook and a positive attitude that inspires others.
- Intellectual curiosity and a philosophical mindset.
- Blunt and straightforward communication, sometimes lacking tact.
- Impulsive decision-making and a tendency to take risks.
- Generous and supportive, always willing to lend a helping hand.
- Restlessness and a constant need for change and new experiences.

PERSONALITY OF CAPRICORN

The personality of Capricorn is characterized by several key traits. Capricorns are known for their ambition, determination, and strong work ethic. They possess a practical and disciplined nature, always striving for success and achieving their goals. They are responsible and reliable individuals who take their commitments seriously.

Capricorns are highly organized and structured, preferring order and stability in their lives. They have a natural ability to plan and strategize, making them excellent managers and leaders. They approach tasks with a methodical mindset and are known for their attention to detail.

While they may appear serious and reserved on the surface, Capricorns have a dry sense of humor and can lighten the mood when appropriate. They are practical and pragmatic, always looking for the most efficient way to solve problems and make decisions.

Capricorns value tradition and respect authority. They are typically cautious and prefer to take calculated risks rather than impulsive actions. Their disciplined nature extends to their personal lives, as they often prioritize their responsibilities and may sometimes appear reserved or guarded in their emotions.

Capricorns have a deep need for achievement and recognition. They strive to climb the ladder of success and attain social status and financial security. However, they can also be overly critical of themselves and others, setting high standards that can be challenging to meet.

In relationships, Capricorns are loyal and committed partners. They value stability and security and seek long-term connections. While they may take time to open up emotionally, once they do, they are devoted and protective of their loved ones.

Overall, Capricorns are driven, practical, and responsible individuals who excel in their careers and personal endeavors. They possess the determination and discipline to overcome challenges and achieve their goals, making them natural leaders and reliable companions.

WEAKNESSES OF CAPRICORN

Capricorn individuals, while possessing many admirable qualities, are not without their weaknesses. One of their notable weaknesses is a tendency to be overly cautious and conservative. They can sometimes be resistant to change and may have difficulty stepping out of their comfort zones. This can limit their willingness to take risks and explore new opportunities, potentially hindering their personal growth and adaptability.

Another weakness of Capricorn is their tendency to be overly focused on work and success. They can become so absorbed in their professional pursuits that they neglect other aspects of their lives, such as relationships and personal well-being. This can lead to feelings of isolation and a lack of work-life balance, impacting their overall happiness and fulfillment.

Additionally, Capricorn individuals may struggle with perfectionism and self-criticism. They have high standards for themselves and can be overly critical when they fall short of their own expectations. This self-imposed pressure can create unnecessary stress and hinder their ability to fully enjoy their achievements.

It's important to note that these weaknesses are not inherent flaws but rather areas where Capricorn individuals may need to be mindful and work on personal growth. By embracing change, finding a healthy work-life balance, and practicing self-compassion, Capricorn can develop a more balanced and fulfilling approach to life.

RELATIONSHIP COMPATIBILITY WITH CAPRICORN

Based only on their Sun signs, this is how Capricorn interacts with others. These are the compatibility interpretations for all 12 potential Capricorn combinations. This is a limited and insufficient method of determining compatibility.

However, Sun-sign compatibility remains the foundation for overall harmony in a relationship.

The general rule is that yin and yang do not get along. Yin complements yin, and yang complements yang. While yin and yang partnerships can be successful, they require more effort. Earth and water zodiac signs are both Yin. Yang is represented by the fire and air zodiac signs.

Capricorn (Yin) and Aries (Yang):

When Capricorn and Aries come together, their contrasting energies can create a dynamic and complementary partnership. Capricorn's practicality and ambition can balance Aries' enthusiasm and

9

impulsiveness. They can inspire each other to achieve their goals and create a solid foundation for their relationship. However, conflicts may arise due to Capricorn's cautious nature conflicting with Aries' desire for immediate action. With open communication and compromise, they can build a relationship based on mutual respect and shared ambitions.

Capricorn (Yin) and Taurus (Yin):

The union of Capricorn and Taurus brings together two grounded and reliable individuals. They both value stability, security, and long-term commitments, which forms a strong basis for their relationship. Their shared work ethic and practicality allow them to create a harmonious home environment and work towards shared financial goals. However, both signs can be stubborn and resistant to change, which may lead to occasional conflicts. By nurturing patience and understanding, they can cultivate a steady and enduring partnership.

Capricorn (Yin) and Gemini (Yang):

Capricorn and Gemini have different approaches to life, which can create a unique dynamic in their relationship. Capricorn is practical and focused, while Gemini is curious and adaptable. They can learn from each other, with Capricorn providing stability and structure, and Gemini bringing spontaneity and intellectual stimulation. However, their differing communication styles and priorities may require effort to find common ground. By embracing flexibility and compromise, they can create a relationship that balances stability and excitement.

Capricorn (Yin) and Cancer (Yin):

When Capricorn and Cancer come together, they form a solid and nurturing partnership. Both signs value commitment, family, and security, creating a strong foundation for a long-lasting relationship. Capricorn's ambition and Cancer's emotional depth can complement each other well. However, conflicts may arise from Capricorn's practicality clashing with Cancer's sensitivity. By fostering open communication and empathy, they can navigate these differences and build a loving and supportive bond.

Capricorn (Yin) and Leo (Yang)

The combination of Capricorn and Leo brings together ambition and self-confidence. Capricorn's practicality and determination can inspire Leo's creative pursuits and encourage their personal growth. However, conflicts may arise due to Capricorn's reserved nature contrasting with Leo's desire for attention and recognition. Finding a balance between their individual needs and supporting each other's goals is key to a successful partnership.

Capricorn (Yin) and Virgo (Yin)

When Capricorn and Virgo join forces, they create a grounded and harmonious relationship. Both signs share a practical and detail-oriented approach to life, valuing stability and hard work. They have similar goals and can collaborate effectively, making them a formidable team. However, their perfectionist tendencies may lead to overcritical attitudes towards themselves and each other. By fostering self-acceptance and practicing open communication, they can create a supportive and productive partnership.

Capricorn (Yin) and Libra (Yang):

The union of Capricorn and Libra combines practicality and harmony. Capricorn's realistic approach is balanced by Libra's diplomatic and social nature. They can learn from each other, with Capricorn teaching Libra about responsibility, and Libra bringing balance and refinement to Capricorn's life. However, conflicts may arise from Capricorn's seriousness conflicting with Libra's desire for fun and socializing.

By finding common interests and compromising, they can build a relationship based on mutual respect and shared values.

Capricorn (Yin) and Scorpio (Yin):

Capricorn and Scorpio create a powerful and intense partnership. Both signs are determined and driven, making them a formidable team. They share a deep understanding of each other's ambitions and can support each other's growth. However, conflicts may arise from Capricorn's reserved nature contrasting with Scorpio's passionate intensity. Trust and honesty are crucial in navigating these differences and building a relationship based on mutual respect and loyalty.

Capricorn (Yin) and Sagittarius (Yang):

Capricorn and Sagittarius have different approaches to life, which can bring both challenges and growth opportunities. Capricorn is practical and focused, while Sagittarius is adventurous and spontaneous. They can learn from each other, with Capricorn providing stability and Sagittarius bringing excitement and optimism. However, conflicts may arise from Capricorn's cautious nature conflicting with Sagittarius' desire for freedom. By embracing compromise and open-mindedness, they can create a relationship that balances stability and exploration.

Capricorn (Yin) and Capricorn (Yin):

When two Capricorn individuals come together, they create a relationship built on mutual understanding and shared values. They both value stability, ambition, and hard work, creating a strong foundation for their partnership. However, conflicts may arise from their tendency to be overly serious and work-focused. Finding a healthy work-life balance and prioritizing their emotional connection is essential to maintaining a fulfilling and harmonious relationship.

Capricorn (Yin) and Aquarius (Yang):

Capricorn and Aquarius bring different energies to their relationship. Capricorn is grounded and practical, while Aquarius is innovative and independent. They can complement each other, with Capricorn providing stability and structure, and Aquarius bringing new ideas and perspectives. However, conflicts may arise due to Capricorn's need for tradition and Aquarius' desire for freedom and individuality. Finding a balance between their differing needs and respecting each other's independence is key to a successful partnership.

14

Capricorn (Yin) and Pisces (Yin):

Capricorn and Pisces create a gentle and supportive partnership. Capricorn's practicality and Pisces' emotional depth can balance each other well. They can provide stability and security for each other, fostering a sense of trust and understanding. However, conflicts may arise from Capricorn's realistic approach conflicting with Pisces' dreamy nature. By nurturing empathy and creating a safe space for emotional expression, they can build a loving and nurturing bond.

LOVE AND PASSION

Capricorn individuals approach love and passion with a practical and patient mindset. They value stability, loyalty, and commitment in their relationships. While they may not be overtly expressive or romantic, Capricorns show their love through actions and consistency.

In love, Capricorns are dependable partners who prioritize the long-term aspects of a relationship. They seek a deep and meaningful connection with their partner, built on trust and shared values. Capricorns are highly selective in choosing their romantic partners and are often attracted to individuals who share their ambition and drive.

When it comes to passion, Capricorns may initially appear reserved or cautious. However, beneath their composed exterior lies a strong sensual nature. They are capable of intense physical and emotional connections with their partners. Capricorns value quality over quantity and prefer to build a strong foundation of trust and emotional intimacy before fully expressing their passion.

Capricorns appreciate stability and routine in their love lives, as it provides them with a sense of security. They are willing to invest time and effort into creating a stable and harmonious home environment for themselves and their partners. Capricorns are diligent in their efforts to maintain the romance and passion in their relationships, often finding creative ways to keep the spark alive.

However, Capricorns may sometimes struggle with vulnerability and expressing their emotions. They tend to prioritize their work and responsibilities, which can sometimes create challenges in balancing their personal and romantic lives. Capricorns may need reassurance from their partners that they are valued and loved to help them open up emotionally.

Overall, Capricorns bring stability, loyalty, and a steadfast commitment to their relationships. Their love and passion may be understated, but they make up for it with their unwavering dedication and reliability. When a Capricorn finds a partner who appreciates their grounded nature and supports their ambitions, they can build a lasting and fulfilling love story together.

MARRIAGE

Capricorn individuals approach marriage with a serious and practical mindset. They view it as a long-term commitment and strive to build a solid foundation for their union. Before entering into marriage, Capricorns often prioritize establishing a stable financial position, as financial security is essential to them.

In a marriage, Capricorns value loyalty, dependability, and responsibility. They are dedicated partners who take their marital vows seriously. However, it is important for Capricorns to be mindful of their tendency to become overly critical or argumentative. They should temper their inclination to dispute and criticize, as it can undermine their partner's morale and put the relationship at risk. Effective communication and a willingness to address conflicts constructively are key for a successful marriage with a Capricorn.

Capricorns are committed to making their marriage work and will go to great lengths to ensure its success. They are known for their perseverance and determination, which they apply to all aspects of their lives, including their relationship. However, if Capricorns find that the disagreements within the marriage become insurmountable or compromise their core values, they will not hesitate to consider ending the relationship. They prioritize their own happiness and well-being, recognizing that a healthy and fulfilling marriage requires mutual understanding and compatibility.

In a marriage with a Capricorn, compatibility with a Virgo partner can bring additional harmony. Virgo women, known for their adaptability, have a natural ability to balance work and family duties. They appreciate order, efficiency, and organization in their marriage, approaching their marital responsibilities with a positive attitude and a strong work ethic. Virgo males also value their roles as parents and husbands, and they actively contribute to the household responsibilities. They uphold a sense of equality and fairness in their partnership, ensuring that their spouse never performs more than their fair share.

Overall, a marriage with a Capricorn is characterized by dedication, stability, and a focus on building a secure future. It requires mutual respect, effective communication, and a willingness to work through challenges together. When both partners share common goals and values, a Capricorn marriage can thrive and become a lasting source of fulfillment and support for both individuals.

CHAPTER TWO

CAPRICORN 2024 HOROSCOPE

Overview Capricorn 2024

Dear Capricorn, as you step into the year 2024, the cosmos is aligning in a way that will shape your journey in profound ways. The planetary movements throughout the year indicate a time of opportunities, challenges, and growth. The alignment of the Sun, Mercury, Venus, Mars, and Jupiter will play a crucial role in various aspects of your life, including your career, relationships, health, and personal development.

The year 2024 will be a dynamic year for your career. The Sun's opposition to Jupiter in December suggests a time of expansion and growth in your professional life. You may find yourself taking on new responsibilities or stepping into a leadership role. However, this growth will not come without its challenges. The square between Mercury and Saturn in November indicates potential obstacles that will require careful planning and decision-making. You may need to make tough decisions or navigate difficult conversations at work. However, these challenges will ultimately lead to growth and development in your career.

Financially, the sextile between Venus and Saturn in November indicates stability and potential growth in your financial situation. This is a good time to invest or save money. However, the square between Venus and Uranus in August suggests potential unexpected expenses or financial changes. It's important to be prepared for these potential fluctuations and to manage your finances wisely.

In terms of relationships and social life, the opposition between Venus and Mars in July suggests potential conflicts or disagreements in your personal relationships. These conflicts may stem from differences in values or desires. However, these challenges will provide opportunities for growth and understanding. It's a time to practice patience and empathy and to work on improving your communication skills.

The square between Venus and Neptune in June indicates a time of confusion or misunderstanding in your relationships. You may find yourself questioning your relationships or feeling unsure about your feelings. It's important to communicate clearly and honestly during this time and to seek clarity when needed.

The sesquiquadrate between the Sun and Chiron in June suggests a time of healing and recovery in terms of your health. This is a good time to focus on self-care and wellness practices. You may find yourself drawn to healing modalities such as yoga, meditation, or therapy. The trine between the Sun and Mars in July indicates a period of high energy and vitality. This is a great time to engage in physical activities or to start a new fitness regimen.

The year 2024 will be a significant year for your spiritual growth and personal development. The conjunction between Venus and Pluto in July suggests a time of deep transformation and personal growth. You may find yourself questioning your beliefs or values and seeking a deeper understanding of your purpose in life. This is a time to embrace change and to allow yourself to grow and evolve.

The quintile between Jupiter and Saturn in May suggests a time of spiritual learning and growth. You may find yourself drawn to philosophical or spiritual studies that can help you understand the world in a deeper way. This is a time to explore new ideas and perspectives and to open your mind to new possibilities.

In conclusion, Capricorn, the year 2024 will be a year of growth, transformation, and self-discovery. While there will be challenges along the way, these challenges will provide opportunities for personal development and understanding. Embrace the journey and make the most of the opportunities that come your way. Stay open to learning and growing, and don't be afraid to explore new paths. Your adventurous spirit will guide you through the ups and downs of the year, leading you to new heights in your personal and professional life.

Remember, the stars are merely guides. You have the power to shape your destiny. Use the insights from your horoscope to navigate the year, but always listen to your inner voice. It is your most reliable guide.

Here's to a year filled with growth, success, and happiness.

January 2024

Horoscope

In January 2024, Capricorn individuals will experience a month filled with opportunities and challenges across various aspects of their lives. The planetary aspects during this time emphasize the need for balance, self-reflection, and adaptation. It is essential for Capricorns to remain focused, practical, and resilient in navigating the energies of this month.

The month begins with Venus squaring Saturn on January 1st, which sets the tone for a need to find harmony between desires and responsibilities. Capricorns may feel the tension between their personal ambitions and the obligations they have towards their loved ones or work.

On January 3rd, Venus forms a quincunx with Jupiter, creating a need for adjustments in matters of love and relationships. Capricorns may find themselves torn between their own desires and the expectations of their partners. It is important to communicate openly and find compromises to maintain harmony.

Mercury's quintile with Saturn on the same day enhances Capricorns' intellectual abilities, promoting strategic thinking and effective communication. This aspect supports their career endeavors and encourages seeking guidance from experienced individuals.

Throughout the month, the aspects continue to highlight the importance of self-reflection and finding a balance between personal and professional spheres. Capricorns should pay attention to their intuition and dreams, as the Sun's quintile with Neptune on January 3rd enhances their creative and intuitive abilities.

On January 6th, the Sun squares Chiron, bringing potential challenges related to self-expression. Capricorns may need to confront their fears and insecurities in order to fully express themselves and embrace their unique qualities.

These aspects lay the foundation for a transformative month, where Capricorns have the opportunity to grow and evolve in various areas of their lives. It is crucial to remain grounded, adaptable, and willing to make necessary adjustments to make the most of the energies present.

Love

In January 2024, love and relationships for Capricorn individuals are influenced by a mix of challenging and harmonious aspects. Venus, the planet of love, squares Saturn on January 1st, indicating potential conflicts and limitations within relationships. Capricorns may feel the need to balance their personal desires with their responsibilities and commitments to their partners.

On January 3rd, Venus forms a quincunx with Jupiter, bringing a need for adjustments and compromises in matters of the heart. Capricorns may find themselves torn between their own needs and the expectations of their partners. It is important to communicate openly and honestly to find a middle ground that satisfies both parties.

Throughout the month, the aspects suggest the importance of self-reflection and introspection in relationships. Capricorns may need to reassess their own desires, values, and expectations from a partnership. It is essential to be patient and understanding with their loved ones, allowing for growth and transformation within the relationship.

The trine between Venus and Chiron on January 11th brings opportunities for emotional healing and deepening connections with loved ones. Capricorns may find solace in nurturing relationships and addressing any emotional wounds that may have hindered the relationship's growth.

Communication plays a crucial role in maintaining harmony in relationships during this month. Mercury's aspects, such as the quintile with Saturn and the trine with Jupiter, support effective communication and understanding. Capricorns should make an effort to express their feelings and thoughts clearly, while also being receptive to their partner's needs.

Career

The planetary aspects during this month highlight ambition, strategic thinking, and the need for practical decision-making. Capricorns are encouraged to take advantage of these energies to advance in their professional lives.

Mercury's quintile with Saturn on January 3rd enhances Capricorns' intellectual abilities and promotes strategic thinking. This aspect allows them to communicate effectively and seek guidance from experienced individuals. It is a favorable time for networking and forming beneficial professional connections.

The trine between Mars and Jupiter on January 12th amplifies Capricorns' ambition and drive for success. This aspect supports their career growth, bringing recognition and advancement opportunities.

Capricorns should take calculated risks and seize new opportunities with confidence and determination.

Throughout the month, it is important for Capricorns to stay focused, disciplined, and committed to their goals. The square between Mercury and Neptune on January 8th reminds them to verify information and remain grounded in decision-making processes. Attention to detail and careful planning will be crucial in navigating potential challenges.

Capricorns should also be mindful of the potential power struggles indicated by Venus' semi-square with Pluto on January 10th. Diplomacy, empathy, and assertiveness will be essential in handling conflicts and maintaining a harmonious work environment.

Collaboration and teamwork are emphasized during this month. The trine between Mercury and Jupiter on January 19th promotes positive interactions and opportunities for joint projects. Capricorns should be open to learning from others and sharing their knowledge and expertise.

Finance

January 2024 brings both opportunities and challenges in the financial realm for Capricorn individuals. The planetary aspects during this month highlight the need for careful planning, practicality, and adaptability to make the most of the financial energies present.

Venus squares Saturn on January 1st, which indicates potential financial constraints and limitations. Capricorns may need to exercise caution in their spending and prioritize their financial responsibilities over personal desires.

On January 10th, Venus semi-squares Pluto, bringing potential power struggles and intense emotions related to finances. Capricorns should be mindful of power dynamics in financial dealings and avoid impulsive or risky investments. It is important to seek advice from trusted financial advisors or professionals before making significant financial decisions.

Throughout the month, Capricorns are advised to maintain a balanced approach to their finances. The trine between Venus and Jupiter on January 8th brings opportunities for financial growth and abundance. Capricorns may experience increased financial stability and gains through wise investments or business ventures.

However, the square between Venus and Neptune on January 19th reminds Capricorns to be cautious of unrealistic financial expectations or deceptive financial opportunities. It is important to carefully evaluate all financial transactions and avoid impulsive decisions.

31

Capricorns are encouraged to focus on long-term financial planning and set realistic goals. The aspects of Mercury with Saturn and Jupiter on January 8th and January 19th, respectively, support strategic financial decision-making and the potential for financial growth through careful analysis and informed investments.

Budgeting and financial discipline are crucial during this month. Capricorns should review their financial commitments, cut unnecessary expenses, and focus on building a strong financial foundation for the future.

By maintaining a practical and cautious approach to finances, Capricorn individuals can navigate the financial energies of January and set themselves up for long-term financial stability and success.

Health

The planetary aspects during this month emphasize the importance of self-care, balance, and moderation to maintain optimal health.

The semi-square between the Sun and Saturn on January 9th serves as a reminder for Capricorns to prioritize self-care and avoid overexertion. It is essential to find a balance between work and rest, ensuring that they allocate sufficient time for relaxation and rejuvenation.

The square between Mars and Chiron on January 25th highlights potential physical or emotional vulnerabilities. Capricorns may need to address any lingering health issues or emotional wounds to maintain overall well-being. Seeking professional guidance or support from loved ones can aid in the healing process.

Capricorns should pay attention to their stress levels and find healthy outlets for stress management. Engaging in regular exercise, practicing relaxation techniques, and incorporating self-care activities into their daily routines will contribute to their overall well-being.

The aspects of the Sun with Neptune on January 15th and the Sun with Chiron on January 24th enhance Capricorns' intuitive and spiritual well-being. It is important for them to listen to their inner guidance and prioritize their emotional and spiritual needs.

Diet and nutrition play a significant role in Capricorns' health during this month. It is advisable for them to adopt a balanced and nutritious diet, incorporating fresh fruits, vegetables, and whole foods. Staying hydrated and avoiding excessive consumption of unhealthy foods or substances will contribute to their overall well-being.

Regular check-ups with healthcare professionals are also recommended. Capricorns should ensure they schedule necessary medical appointments and follow through with recommended treatments or therapies.

By prioritizing self-care, stress management, and maintaining a healthy lifestyle, Capricorn individuals can navigate January with improved physical and mental well-being.

Travel

In January 2024, Capricorn individuals may have opportunities for travel, exploration, or a change of scenery. The planetary aspects during this month highlight the need for careful planning, adaptability, and open-mindedness in travel experiences.

The square between Venus and Saturn on January 1st suggests potential delays or limitations in travel plans. Capricorns may need to be flexible and patient when it comes to travel arrangements. It is advisable to have contingency plans and alternative options in place.

The aspects of Venus with Jupiter on January 8th and Venus with Uranus on January 19th bring favorable energies for travel. Capricorns may experience unexpected opportunities for exciting and enjoyable trips. It is important to embrace these opportunities and explore new horizons.

Capricorns should consider incorporating elements of adventure and spontaneity in their travel plans. Exploring new destinations, trying new experiences, and immersing themselves in different cultures will be rewarding.

It is essential for Capricorns to balance their travel aspirations with their responsibilities and commitments. The aspects of Mercury with Saturn and Jupiter on January 8th and January 19th, respectively, encourage practical planning and mindful decision-making in travel arrangements.

During travel, Capricorns should prioritize self-care and ensure they maintain a healthy routine. Adequate rest, proper nutrition, and hydration are essential to sustain energy levels during trips.

Open-mindedness and adaptability are key qualities for Capricorns during their travels. Unexpected events or changes in plans may occur, and it is important to approach them with a positive and flexible mindset.

Capricorns should also make an effort to connect with locals and immerse themselves in the culture and traditions of the places they visit. Building meaningful connections and gaining unique insights will enrich their travel experiences.

By embracing opportunities for travel, planning mindfully, and staying open to new experiences, Capricorn individuals can have fulfilling and memorable journeys in January 2024.

Insight from the stars

The stars highlight the importance of open communication, strategic thinking, and practical decision-making. By embracing the transformative energies of this month and staying focused on their goals, Capricorns can lay a solid foundation for long-term success and growth in various aspects of their lives.

Best days of the month: January 6th, 12th, 19th, 21st, 25th, 28th, and 30th.

February 2024

Horoscope

The planetary aspects during this month highlight the need for adaptability, self-reflection, and strategic decision-making.

The semi-square between Mars and Saturn on February 2nd may present some challenges and obstacles. Capricorns are advised to exercise patience and perseverance in overcoming any setbacks they encounter. It is important to remain focused on their long-term goals and not be discouraged by temporary obstacles.

The conjunction of Mercury and Pluto on February 5th brings intense intellectual energy and the potential for profound insights. Capricorns may find themselves delving deep into their thoughts and gaining clarity on important matters. This aspect encourages them to embrace their inner power and use it to make transformative changes in their lives.

The trine between Venus and Uranus on February 7th brings excitement and spontaneity to Capricorn's love life. It is a favorable time for new romantic connections, exploring unconventional relationships, and breaking free from old patterns. Capricorns should embrace their adventurous side and be open to unexpected love opportunities.

The stars advise Capricorns to embrace change and transformation during February. By staying adaptable, focused, and open to new possibilities, they can make the most of the dynamic energies present and pave the way for personal and professional growth.

Love

The planetary aspects during this month highlight the need for self-reflection, emotional growth, and embracing unconventional relationships.

The square between Venus and Chiron on February 5th may bring up past wounds or insecurities in love relationships. Capricorns should take this opportunity to address any emotional baggage, heal old wounds, and nurture their emotional well-being. It is a time for self-love and self-acceptance.

The conjunction of Venus and Mars on February 22nd ignites passion, desire, and a sense of adventure in Capricorn's love life. This aspect brings excitement and spontaneity, encouraging Capricorns to explore new romantic connections and express their desires with confidence.

Capricorns are encouraged to step out of their comfort zones and embrace unconventional relationships or experiences. The sextile between Venus and Uranus on February 7th supports Capricorns in breaking free from old patterns and embracing their authentic selves in love. This aspect brings opportunities for unexpected and exhilarating connections.

Communication and emotional vulnerability play significant roles in maintaining healthy relationships. The sextile between Mercury and Chiron on February 15th enhances Capricorns' ability to express their emotions and connect on a deeper level with their partners. It is an ideal time for heartfelt conversations and addressing any unresolved emotional issues.

Single Capricorns may find themselves drawn to unconventional or non-traditional relationships during this month. The conjunction of Venus and Mars on February 22nd brings opportunities for passionate and exciting encounters. It is important for Capricorns to trust their instincts, follow their desires, and be open to new possibilities.

For those in committed relationships, the energy of February encourages growth and transformation. Capricorns should embrace honest communication, work through any challenges, and foster a sense of adventure in their partnerships. The sextile between

Venus and True Node on February 29th supports the growth and evolution of long-term relationships.

Career

February 2024 holds significant opportunities and growth potential for Capricorns in their professional lives. The planetary aspects during this month highlight the need for strategic thinking, adaptability, and taking calculated risks.

The sextile between Mercury and Jupiter on February 16th brings favorable energies for career advancement and expansion. Capricorns may find themselves presented with new opportunities, promotions, or recognition for their hard work and dedication. It is essential for them to showcase their skills, communicate their ideas confidently, and seize the moment to make significant strides in their careers.

Capricorns should embrace their ambitious nature and aim high in setting their career goals. The conjunction of Venus and Mars on February 22nd encourages Capricorns to take calculated risks and pursue new ventures. It is a time to harness their inner drive, be proactive, and embrace challenges with confidence.

Collaboration and networking play a crucial role in Capricorn's career success during this month. The sextile between Mercury and True Node on February 15th enhances their ability to build meaningful connections and alliances. Capricorns should seek opportunities to collaborate with like-minded individuals, share their ideas, and tap into the collective wisdom around them.

It is important for Capricorns to maintain a balance between their professional ambitions and personal well-being. The semi-square between Mars and Saturn on February 2nd reminds them to avoid overexertion and prioritize self-care. Finding a harmonious work-life balance will contribute to their overall productivity and long-term success.

Financial stability and discipline are also important considerations in Capricorn's career journey. The square between Venus and Jupiter on February 24th cautions against impulsive spending or risky financial decisions. Capricorns should approach their finances with caution, make wise investments, and focus on long-term financial stability.

Finance

February 2024 brings a mixed financial outlook for Capricorns. The planetary aspects during this month highlight the importance of careful planning, disciplined spending, and strategic decision-making.

Capricorns should exercise caution in their financial matters, particularly in the face of impulsive or risky investments. The square between Venus and Jupiter on February 24th serves as a reminder to avoid impulsive spending and to focus on long-term financial stability. It is advisable for Capricorns to seek professional financial advice before making significant financial decisions.

The sextile between Venus and Uranus on February 7th brings unexpected opportunities for financial growth and innovation. Capricorns may encounter unique and unconventional avenues for generating income or expanding their financial portfolio. It is important for them to stay open-minded, seize these opportunities, and evaluate the risks involved.

Capricorns should also focus on building a solid foundation for their financial future. The conjunction of Venus and Mars on February 22nd encourages them to take calculated risks and pursue new ventures. It is a favorable time for Capricorns to strategize and make bold financial moves that align with their long-term goals.

The sextile between Mercury and Jupiter on February 16th brings favorable energies for financial growth and prosperity. Capricorns may experience increased income, successful negotiations, or favorable financial deals. It is crucial for them to leverage their communication skills, think strategically, and seize opportunities for financial advancement.

Maintaining financial discipline and budgeting are essential for Capricorns during this month. They should prioritize saving, track their expenses, and avoid unnecessary expenditures. Creating a solid financial plan and sticking to it will ensure long-term financial stability.

Health

In February 2024, Capricorns need to prioritize their physical and emotional well-being. The planetary aspects during this month highlight the importance of self-care, stress management, and maintaining a healthy balance.

Capricorns may experience fluctuations in their energy levels and emotional state. The semi-square between Mars and Saturn on February 2nd reminds them to avoid overexertion and to find a balance between work and rest. It is crucial for Capricorns to listen to their bodies, get enough sleep, and recharge their energy reserves.

Emotional well-being plays a significant role in overall health. The conjunction of Venus and Mars on February 22nd brings heightened emotions and passion. Capricorns should pay attention to their emotional needs, practice self-care, and seek healthy outlets for their feelings. Engaging in activities like meditation, journaling, or seeking support from loved ones can contribute to their emotional well-being.

Capricorns should also be mindful of their stress levels during this month. The square between Venus and Jupiter on February 24th cautions against excessive stress and the potential impact on their physical health. It is essential for Capricorns to practice stress-management techniques such as exercise, meditation, or engaging in hobbies that bring joy and relaxation.

Taking care of their physical health is of utmost importance. Capricorns should prioritize regular exercise and maintaining a balanced diet. The sextile between Mercury and True Node on February 15th supports their ability to make informed choices about their health and well-being. Capricorns may benefit from seeking professional advice on nutrition and incorporating holistic practices into their lifestyle.

It is also important for Capricorns to address any lingering health concerns or seek preventive care. The conjunction of Venus and Mars on February 22nd brings an opportunity for Capricorns to take charge of their health and schedule necessary medical check-ups or consultations.

Travel

February 2024 presents exciting opportunities for travel and exploration for Capricorns. The planetary aspects during this month highlight the potential for spontaneous and adventurous trips, as well as the need for careful planning and flexibility.

The conjunction of Venus and Mars on February 22nd brings a sense of adventure and wanderlust to Capricorns' travel plans. It is a favorable time for them to embrace their spontaneous side and seek new experiences. Capricorns may feel drawn to unique and off-the-beaten-path destinations, allowing them to broaden their horizons and expand their perspectives.

Capricorns should be open to unexpected travel opportunities that may arise. The sextile between Venus and Uranus on February 7th brings the potential for spontaneous trips or last-minute invitations. It is important for Capricorns to stay flexible and adaptable, as these opportunities may bring exciting and memorable experiences.

However, careful planning is still essential for a smooth travel experience. Capricorns should consider practical aspects such as transportation, accommodation, and budgeting. The conjunction of Venus and Mars on February 22nd encourages them to make calculated and strategic decisions when it comes to travel arrangements. Researching destinations, creating itineraries, and being prepared for any contingencies will ensure a stress-free travel experience.

Capricorns should also prioritize self-care during their travels. The square between Venus and Jupiter on February 24th reminds them to strike a balance between exploration and rest. It is important for Capricorns to take breaks, engage in self-care activities, and avoid overexertion. Listening to their bodies and finding moments of relaxation and rejuvenation will enhance their overall travel experience.

During their travels, Capricorns may also have the opportunity to connect with people from different cultures and backgrounds. The sextile between Mercury and True Node on February 15th supports their ability to communicate and form meaningful connections. Engaging in conversations with locals, learning about different customs, and embracing cultural experiences will enrich their travel journeys.

Insight from the stars

Capricorns are advised to embrace change, be open to new possibilities, and trust their instincts. The planetary aspects during this month highlight the importance of navigating through challenges and seizing the abundant opportunities that comes your way.

Best days of the month: February 7th, 15th, 16th, 22nd, 24th, and 29th

March 2024

Horoscope

In March 2024, Capricorns will experience a dynamic and transformative month, both personally and professionally. The planetary aspects during this period indicate a time of growth, self-reflection, and taking bold steps towards achieving their goals.

Capricorns will feel a heightened sense of intuition and emotional depth. The conjunction of the Sun and Neptune on March 17th brings spiritual awareness and encourages Capricorns to delve into their inner selves. It is a time for self-reflection, meditation, and exploring their spiritual beliefs. By connecting with their intuition, Capricorns can gain valuable insights that will guide them on their path.

March is a month of growth, self-reflection, and progress for Capricorns. By embracing their intuition, focusing on their career goals, managing their finances wisely, prioritizing their health, and nurturing their relationships, Capricorns can make significant strides towards their desired outcomes.

Love

For Capricorns in committed relationships, the conjunction of Venus and Saturn on March 21st brings a sense of stability, commitment, and long-term planning. It is a favorable time to discuss shared goals, deepen emotional bonds, and solidify the foundations of the relationship. Capricorns should focus on open and honest communication, demonstrating their dedication to their partner, and nurturing the emotional connection between them.

Single Capricorns may find themselves drawn to more serious and meaningful connections. The conjunction of Venus and Saturn on March 21st encourages them to seek partnerships that align with their long-term goals and values. It is important for single Capricorns to remain patient and not settle for superficial connections. Taking time for self-reflection, understanding personal needs and desires, and being open to new possibilities will pave the way for a fulfilling and committed relationship.

Emotional depth and vulnerability play a significant role in Capricorns' love lives during this period. The semi-square between Venus and Chiron on March 14th reminds Capricorns to address any emotional wounds or insecurities that may hinder their ability to fully connect with others. By engaging in self-healing practices, seeking support, and embracing their vulnerability, Capricorns can create deeper and more authentic connections with their partners.

Capricorns should also prioritize quality time and nurturing gestures in their relationships. The sextile between Venus and Jupiter on March 24th enhances romantic experiences, encourages acts of kindness, and promotes a sense of adventure and joy within partnerships. Planning meaningful dates, expressing love and appreciation, and exploring new activities together will strengthen the bond between Capricorns and their partners.

Career

The conjunction of Venus and Saturn on March 21st highlights the need for hard work and commitment in the professional realm. Capricorns should focus on building a solid foundation, demonstrating their reliability, and taking on responsibilities that showcase their skills and expertise. This is an opportune time to seek recognition for their efforts and showcase their leadership abilities.

Capricorns should also take advantage of networking opportunities and seek guidance from mentors or professionals in their field. The semi-sextile between Mercury and Uranus on March 22nd encourages Capricorns to think outside the box, embrace innovation, and explore new ideas or approaches to their work. Collaborating with like-minded individuals and expanding their professional network can lead to exciting opportunities and career growth.

Strategic decision-making is crucial during this period. The conjunction of Mercury and True Node on March 18th signifies the need for Capricorns to align their actions with their long-term career goals. It is a favorable time to assess their progress, make necessary adjustments, and set realistic and achievable targets. Capricorns should prioritize tasks, manage their time effectively, and stay organized to maximize their productivity.

The semi-square between Mercury and Mars on March 14th reminds Capricorns to maintain a balanced approach to their work. It is important to avoid impulsive actions or confrontations that may hinder professional relationships. Instead, Capricorns should channel their energy into focused and purposeful endeavors. Embracing teamwork, effective communication, and diplomatic solutions will contribute to a harmonious work environment and facilitate their career progression.

Capricorns should also consider investing in professional development and expanding their skill set. The sextile between Mercury and Jupiter on March 18th favors educational pursuits, attending workshops or conferences, or seeking additional training. By honing their abilities and staying up-to-date with industry trends, Capricorns can position themselves for future success and advancement.

Finance

Capricorns should begin by reviewing their financial situation and identifying any areas that require attention. The semi-square between Venus and Chiron on March 14th reminds Capricorns to address any emotional or psychological factors that may influence their financial habits. By understanding their relationship with money and working towards a healthy mindset, Capricorns can make sound financial decisions.

Budgeting and prudent spending habits are key during this period. The semi-square between Venus and Saturn on March 12th serves as a reminder for Capricorns to be disciplined and conscientious when it comes to their expenses. Creating a budget, tracking their income and expenses, and identifying areas where they can cut back will contribute to their overall financial stability.

Capricorns should also focus on long-term financial planning and investment opportunities. The conjunction of Venus and Saturn on March 21st emphasizes the need for strategic decision-making and a focus on long-term goals. Capricorns should consider consulting with a financial advisor or conducting thorough research before making any significant investments. This is a favorable time to explore avenues for growth, such as real estate, stocks, or retirement savings.

Furthermore, Capricorns should prioritize debt management and clearing any outstanding financial obligations. The semi-square between Venus and Pluto on March 25th urges Capricorns to address any financial burdens head-on. By creating a plan for debt repayment, seeking professional advice if needed, and adopting responsible financial habits, Capricorns can regain control over their financial situation.

It is also essential for Capricorns to maintain a healthy work-life balance and avoid excessive stress related to their finances. The semi-square between Mercury and Mars on March 14th reminds Capricorns to manage their emotions and make financial decisions with a clear and rational mindset.

Health

Capricorns should be mindful of their overall health and pay attention to any signs of stress or fatigue. The conjunction of Venus and Mars on March 22nd may bring about a period of heightened activity and increased demands. It is crucial for Capricorns to listen to their bodies, set realistic boundaries, and prioritize self-care practices such as regular exercise, sufficient rest, and a balanced diet.

Emotional well-being is equally important during this period. The semi-sextile between Venus and Chiron on March 14th encourages Capricorns to address any emotional wounds or unresolved issues that may impact their overall health. Seeking support from loved ones, engaging in therapy or counseling, and practicing self-reflection can contribute to emotional healing and overall well-being.

Capricorns should also be mindful of their stress levels and adopt effective stress management techniques. The semi-square between Mercury and Mars on March 14th serves as a reminder for Capricorns to find healthy outlets for stress, such as meditation, yoga, or engaging in hobbies and activities that bring joy and relaxation. It is essential to create a balance between work and personal life to avoid burnout and maintain optimal health.

Additionally, Capricorns should pay attention to their physical fitness and engage in activities that promote strength and vitality. The conjunction of Mars and Pluto on March 14th signifies a period of heightened energy and determination. Capricorns can channel this energy into physical exercise, exploring new fitness routines, or challenging themselves with new goals. Finding activities that bring enjoyment and a sense of accomplishment will contribute to overall physical well-being.

Capricorns should also focus on maintaining a healthy sleep routine. The semi-sextile between Mercury and Neptune on March 21st reminds Capricorns of the importance of quality rest and rejuvenation. Creating a peaceful sleep environment, practicing relaxation techniques, and ensuring a sufficient amount of sleep each night will enhance overall health and vitality.

Travel

Capricorns should embrace their adventurous spirit and consider planning trips or getaways that offer new experiences. The sextile between Venus and Uranus on March 9th encourages Capricorns to explore unique destinations, engage in cultural activities, and seek out new perspectives. Whether it's a short weekend trip or a more extended vacation, Capricorns should aim to broaden their horizons and immerse themselves in different cultures.

It is advisable for Capricorns to plan their travels in advance and pay attention to practical details. The semi-square between Mercury and Mars on March 14th reminds Capricorns to prioritize thorough research, ensure necessary travel documents are in order, and make arrangements for accommodations and transportation. Being organized and well-prepared will contribute to a smooth and enjoyable travel experience.

Capricorns should also consider incorporating wellness practices into their travel plans. The conjunction of Venus and Neptune on March 21st suggests that trips focused on relaxation, rejuvenation, and spiritual growth can be particularly beneficial. Retreats, wellness resorts, or destinations known for their natural beauty and serene environments can provide Capricorns with the opportunity to recharge and find inner peace.

Additionally, Capricorns should make an effort to connect with locals and engage in cultural exchanges during their travels. The sextile between Mercury and Jupiter on March 22nd encourages Capricorns to seek out authentic experiences, interact with the local community, and embrace new perspectives. Engaging in conversations, trying local cuisine, and participating in cultural events will enrich the travel experience and create lasting memories.

Capricorns should also be mindful of their travel budgets and financial considerations. The semi-square between Venus and Saturn on March 12th reminds Capricorns to plan their expenses carefully and consider practical aspects such as accommodation choices, transportation options, and dining preferences. By being mindful of their finances, Capricorns can enjoy their travels without unnecessary financial stress.

Insight from the stars

Go Stargazing Naked Night: Find a secluded spot on the evening of March 21st, strip down to your birthday suit, and indulge in the awe-inspiring beauty of the night sky. Feel the connection to the cosmos and revel in the freedom of being one with the universe (ensure you choose a legal and appropriate location!).

Best days of the month: March 1st, 9th, 14th, 18th, 21st, 22nd and 25th

April 2024

Horoscope

The month begins with Mercury in Aries forming a semi-sextile with Venus in Pisces, indicating a harmonious blend of communication and emotional expression. This alignment encourages you to seek balance in your relationships and effectively communicate your desires.

The Sun in Aries forms a semi-sextile with Saturn in Pisces, highlighting the importance of discipline and responsibility in your personal and professional life. This combination urges you to find a balance between taking assertive action and maintaining stability.

April 3rd brings a powerful quintile aspect between the Sun and Pluto, inspiring you to delve deep into your inner power and tap into your personal transformation. This alignment encourages you to embrace change and let go of any limiting beliefs or patterns that no longer serve you.

Mars forms a quintile with Uranus on April 3rd, igniting a surge of innovative and creative energy within you. This aspect encourages you to take risks, think outside the box, and pursue unique opportunities that align with your authentic self.

The conjunction between Venus and Neptune in Pisces on April 3rd enhances your emotional sensitivity and intuition in matters of the heart. This alignment brings a dreamy and romantic energy, allowing you to connect on a deeper level with your loved ones.

On April 4th, the Sun conjuncts the True Node in Aries, marking a significant turning point in your life path and destiny. This alignment brings a sense of purpose and clarity, guiding you towards your true calling.

The month continues with various aspects influencing your personal and professional life, encouraging growth and self-discovery. Stay attuned to these celestial energies as they can provide valuable insights and opportunities for personal development.

Love

In matters of the heart, April holds immense potential for Capricorn individuals. The conjunction between Venus and Neptune on April 3rd creates a deeply romantic and enchanting energy, elevating your emotional connections and fostering a sense of spiritual union with your partner. This alignment invites you to explore the depths of your emotions and express your love with authenticity and vulnerability.

For singles, this alignment can bring encounters with captivating and mysterious individuals who resonate with your soul. Pay attention to the subtle cues and trust your intuition when it comes to potential romantic prospects.

However, it's important to maintain a balanced perspective and avoid idealizing love or ignoring any red flags. Take the time to assess the practical aspects of your relationships and ensure that they align with your long-term goals and values.

Communication is key in love relationships during April, as Mercury's presence in Aries encourages open and honest dialogue with your partner. Express your needs and desires while also listening attentively to your partner's concerns. By nurturing effective communication, you can build stronger bonds and resolve any conflicts that may arise.

Career

Career-wise, April presents a mix of challenges and opportunities for Capricorn individuals. The alignment of Mars and Saturn in Pisces on April 10th highlights the importance of discipline, persistence, and strategic planning in your professional endeavors.

This conjunction encourages you to reassess your long-term goals and make necessary adjustments to stay on track. It's a time for laying solid foundations and implementing practical strategies to achieve your ambitions.

While you may encounter obstacles or delays, your determination and hard work will help you overcome them. Embrace the lessons and experiences that come your way, as they will contribute to your growth and development.

Collaborative ventures and networking play a significant role in your career during April. The semi-sextile between the Sun in Aries and Jupiter in Taurus on April 8th fosters positive connections and opportunities for expansion. Seek support from colleagues and mentors, and be open to new partnerships or collaborations that can propel your career forward.

It's crucial to maintain a proactive approach and seize opportunities for professional development. Attend workshops, seminars, or training sessions that enhance your skills and knowledge. By investing in your growth, you will position yourself for future success.

Remember to balance your ambitions with self-care to avoid burnout. Find ways to manage stress and maintain a healthy work-life balance. Regular self-reflection and introspection will help you align your career path with your personal values and aspirations.

Finance

Financial matters require careful attention and planning in April for Capricorn individuals. The conjunction of Venus and Chiron in Aries on April 21st brings a focus on healing and growth in your relationship with money.

This alignment urges you to address any emotional issues or limiting beliefs around finances. It's a favorable time to seek advice from financial professionals or experts who can provide guidance on wealth management and investment opportunities.

April presents an opportunity for financial planning and stability. Evaluate your current financial situation, review your budget, and set realistic goals for the future. Consider long-term investments that align with your financial objectives, ensuring a balance between risk and security.

Be cautious with impulsive spending and avoid making hasty financial decisions. Practice prudence and discipline when it comes to managing your resources. Prioritize your needs over wants and maintain a realistic perspective on your financial capabilities.

Take advantage of the supportive aspects in April, such as the semi-square between Venus and Jupiter on April 8th. This alignment reminds you to find a healthy balance between enjoying your wealth and saving for the future. Consider setting aside a portion of your income for savings or investments, ensuring long-term financial stability.

Remember that true financial security is built on a foundation of sound financial practices, including budgeting, saving, and responsible debt management. Seek financial advice if needed, as professional guidance can provide valuable insights and strategies for building wealth.

By adopting a proactive and balanced approach to your finances, you can navigate the fluctuations of the economy and create a solid foundation for future prosperity. Stay focused, remain disciplined, and make informed financial decisions to achieve your desired financial goals.

Health

Your health and well-being require extra attention and care in April. The presence of Mars in Pisces signifies the importance of taking care of your physical and emotional needs. It's essential to prioritize self-care practices to maintain your overall well-being.

April calls for a holistic approach to health, focusing not only on physical fitness but also on mental and emotional wellness. Incorporate regular exercise into your routine, choosing activities that you enjoy and that nourish your body and mind. Engaging in activities like yoga, meditation, or tai chi can help reduce stress, increase flexibility, and promote overall balance.

Pay attention to your emotional well-being as well. The alignment of Mars and Chiron on April 17th emphasizes the need to address any emotional wounds or traumas that may be affecting your health. Consider seeking therapy or counseling to heal and release any emotional baggage that may be impacting your overall well-being.

Maintain a balanced and nutritious diet to support your physical vitality. Focus on incorporating whole foods, fresh fruits and vegetables, lean proteins, and healthy fats into your meals. Stay hydrated and be mindful of portion sizes to maintain a healthy weight.

Prioritize rest and quality sleep to allow your body to rejuvenate and recharge. Establish a consistent sleep routine and create a relaxing environment conducive to restful sleep.

Be cautious of overworking yourself or taking on too many responsibilities. The demands of your career and personal life can sometimes lead to burnout, so make sure to set boundaries and create time for relaxation and leisure activities.

Listen to your body and give yourself permission to take breaks when needed. Incorporate stress management techniques, such as deep breathing exercises or mindfulness practices, into your daily routine to promote a sense of calm and inner balance.

By nurturing your physical, mental, and emotional well-being, you can enhance your overall health and resilience.

Travel

The alignment of Venus and Jupiter on April 23rd creates a harmonious energy, inspiring you to embark on new adventures and broaden your horizons.

Whether it's for business or pleasure, travel during this time can bring significant benefits. It offers opportunities for personal growth, networking, and expanding your perspective. Embrace the experiences that travel brings, as they can lead to valuable connections and insights.

When planning your trips, consider both your professional and personal goals. Look for destinations that align with your career objectives, providing opportunities for networking or professional development. At the same time, choose locations that offer relaxation and rejuvenation, allowing you to unwind and recharge.

Be open to exploring new cultures, traditions, and cuisines. Engage in local experiences, connect with the local community, and embrace the unique aspects of each destination. This will enrich your travel experience and provide you with a deeper understanding of the world.

Ensure a balance between work and leisure during your trips. Allocate time for relaxation and self-care, allowing yourself to fully enjoy the experience. Connect with nature, engage in outdoor activities, and indulge in the local cuisine to make the most of your travel adventures.

While traveling, stay mindful of your health and safety. Follow any travel advisories or guidelines, and take necessary precautions to protect yourself and others. Carry essential items like hand sanitizers, masks, and any necessary medications to ensure your well-being throughout your journey.

Insight from the stars

Tap into your inner strength and assertiveness, allowing yourself to transcend any obstacles and make remarkable progress. Embrace this cosmic gift, and let it empower you to manifest positive change in all aspects of your life.

Best days of the month: April 3rd, 8th, 10th, 17th, 19th, 21st and 23rd

May 2024

Horoscope

As the month begins, Venus squares Pluto on May 1st, highlighting the potential for intense emotional experiences and power struggles in relationships. This aspect urges you to navigate conflicts with grace and seek resolutions that honor the needs of both parties.

The sextile between Mars and Pluto on May 3rd ignites a surge of personal power and determination within you. This alignment empowers you to overcome obstacles and achieve your goals with unwavering strength. Use this energy to take decisive action and make positive changes in various areas of your life.

On May 7th, the Sun sextiles Saturn, bringing stability and discipline to your endeavors. This alignment supports your efforts in career and personal growth, emphasizing the importance of patience, persistence, and strategic planning.

Mid-May brings a potent conjunction between Venus and Jupiter on May 18th, amplifying love, abundance, and opportunities for expansion. This alignment fosters harmonious relationships and opens

68

doors for financial prosperity. Embrace the blessings and be open to receiving the abundance that the universe offers.

The month concludes with a conjunction between Mars and Chiron on May 29th, marking a significant period of healing and transformation. This aspect encourages you to confront and heal old wounds, allowing you to step into your power and embrace your authenticity.

Throughout May, stay attuned to your intuition and inner guidance. Trust your instincts when making decisions and remain open to the lessons and growth opportunities that come your way. Embrace the transformative energies of the month, and allow them to propel you towards a more empowered and fulfilling future.

Love

Love takes center stage in May for Capricorn individuals, with celestial influences guiding you towards deeper connections and profound emotional experiences. The square between Venus and Pluto on May 1st can bring intense dynamics in relationships, challenging you to navigate power struggles and transform any unhealthy patterns.

Embrace open and honest communication with your partner, allowing for vulnerability and understanding. Work together to find resolutions that honor both individuals' needs and foster a sense of harmony and growth.

The conjunction between Venus and Jupiter on May 18th amplifies the romantic energies, bringing blessings and opportunities for love and abundance. If you're single, this alignment can introduce a significant romantic prospect or deepen an existing connection.

Take time to nurture your relationship, create meaningful experiences together, and express your love and appreciation. Plan romantic outings or surprise gestures that foster emotional connection and intimacy.

For those seeking love, this alignment opens doors for new connections and expands your social circle. Attend social events, engage in activities that align with your interests, and be open to meeting someone special. Trust in the universe's timing, and know that love may come when you least expect it.

Throughout May, remember the importance of self-love and self-care. Nurture your own emotional well-being and maintain a healthy balance between your personal life and your relationship. By taking care of yourself, you'll have more to offer to your partner or potential partners.

Career

May holds significant potential for career growth and professional opportunities for Capricorn individuals. The sextile between Mars and Pluto on May 3rd fuels your ambition and determination, propelling you towards achieving your career goals.

Embrace your inner power and take decisive action. Trust your abilities and don't shy away from challenging projects or leadership roles. Your perseverance and hard work will be recognized and rewarded.

The Sun's sextile with Saturn on May 7th reinforces discipline and stability in your professional endeavors. This alignment emphasizes the importance of careful planning and strategic execution. Take the time to analyze your long-term goals and create a roadmap for success.

Collaboration and networking play a significant role in your career during May. Seek opportunities to connect with colleagues and industry professionals. Attend networking events, conferences, or seminars where you can showcase your skills and expand your professional network.

The conjunction between Venus and Jupiter on May 18th brings blessings and opportunities for financial prosperity. This alignment can attract abundance and success in your career, especially if you're involved in business ventures or negotiations. Be open to new partnerships or collaborations that can expand your professional horizons.

Stay focused on your long-term objectives, but remain adaptable to changes and opportunities that arise. Flexibility and versatility are key qualities that will help you navigate the dynamic energy of the month.

Continue to invest in your professional development and seek opportunities for growth. Take courses, attend workshops, or engage in self-study to enhance your skills and knowledge. Embrace a proactive approach and stay updated with industry trends and advancements.

By harnessing the transformative energies of May, you can make significant strides in your career. Trust your instincts, be open to new possibilities, and seize opportunities that align with your long-term goals. With dedication and strategic planning, success is within your reach.

Finance

May presents both opportunities and challenges when it comes to finances for Capricorn individuals. The square between Venus and Pluto on May 1st brings a need for caution and careful financial management.

Be mindful of power struggles or conflicts that may arise around money matters.

Practice restraint and avoid impulsive spending. Stick to a budget and prioritize your financial goals. Look for ways to cut unnecessary expenses and save for the future.

The conjunction between Venus and Jupiter on May 18th can bring positive financial opportunities and abundance. This alignment favors investments, business partnerships, and financial negotiations. However, exercise caution and ensure you conduct thorough research and seek professional advice before making any major financial decisions.

Take time to review your financial strategies and seek ways to enhance your wealth. Consider long-term investments that align with your financial objectives. Diversify your portfolio and seek expert guidance if needed.

Maintain a disciplined approach to money management. Set realistic financial goals and establish a savings plan. Focus on building an emergency fund and protecting yourself against unexpected expenses.

Consider the long-term implications of your financial decisions. Avoid taking unnecessary risks or indulging in speculative ventures. Prudent financial planning and patience will yield more sustainable results.

Remember to find a balance between enjoying your resources and saving for the future. Allocate a portion of your income towards experiences that bring joy and fulfillment, while also ensuring you're building a solid financial foundation.

Regularly review your financial progress and make adjustments as needed. Seek opportunities to increase your income, whether through career advancements, side projects, or passive income streams. By adopting a proactive and strategic approach to your finances, you can achieve stability and long-term prosperity.

Health

In May, prioritize self-care and well-being to maintain optimal health for Capricorn individuals. The Sun's semi-square with Neptune on May 3rd may bring a temporary dip in energy or susceptibility to fatigue. Ensure you get enough rest and practice self-care activities that rejuvenate your mind, body, and spirit.

Maintaining a balanced and nutritious diet is essential for your well-being. Focus on consuming whole foods, fresh fruits, vegetables, lean proteins, and healthy fats. Stay hydrated and be mindful of portion sizes to support your overall health.

Regular exercise is crucial for your physical and mental well-being. Engage in activities that you enjoy and that promote strength, flexibility, and cardiovascular health. Find a routine that works for you and stick to it, even if it means incorporating shorter workout sessions into your busy schedule.

Mental and emotional well-being are equally important. Practice stress management techniques, such as meditation, deep breathing exercises, or mindfulness practices. Prioritize activities that bring you joy, relaxation, and a sense of fulfillment.

Be mindful of any emotional or mental health concerns that may arise. Seek support from trusted friends, family, or professionals if needed. Addressing any underlying issues allows for greater overall well-being.

Maintain a healthy work-life balance and establish boundaries to prevent burnout. Take breaks, both short and long, to recharge and rejuvenate. Connect with nature, engage in hobbies, or spend quality time with loved ones to nurture your emotional and mental health.

Regular health check-ups and preventive screenings are essential for early detection and prevention of potential health issues. Stay proactive in managing your health and seek professional advice for any concerns or symptoms.

By prioritizing self-care, maintaining a healthy lifestyle, and seeking balance, you can nurture your overall well-being and thrive in May.

Travel

May brings opportunities for travel and exploration for Capricorn individuals. Whether for leisure or business, travel can offer valuable experiences and opportunities for personal growth.

Plan your trips carefully, considering both your personal preferences and your career objectives. Choose destinations that align with your interests and offer opportunities for relaxation, cultural enrichment, and personal development.

The conjunction between Venus and Jupiter on May 18th enhances the positive energy for travel. This alignment encourages you to broaden your horizons, embrace new cultures, and expand your perspective through immersive travel experiences.

When traveling, be open to spontaneity and allow yourself to fully immerse in the local culture. Engage in authentic experiences, try local cuisine, and connect with the local community. Embrace the opportunity to learn and gain a deeper understanding of different cultures and traditions.

Maintain flexibility in your travel plans, as unexpected changes or opportunities may arise. Be prepared for potential delays or disruptions and have contingency plans in place. Travel insurance can provide additional peace of mind and protection during your journeys.

During your trips, prioritize self-care and well-being. Take breaks to rest and recharge, especially if your travel itinerary is packed. Balance exploration with relaxation, ensuring you have time to rejuvenate and enjoy the experience fully.

Stay mindful of your health and safety while traveling. Follow any travel advisories or guidelines, and take necessary precautions to protect yourself and others. Stay informed about the local customs, laws, and regulations of your destination to ensure a smooth and enjoyable travel experience.

Embrace the transformative energies of travel and allow them to expand your horizons, deepen your understanding of the world, and foster personal growth.

Insight from the stars

Embrace the adventurous spirit and let your hair down. Engage in activities that bring you joy and spontaneity. Allow yourself to take calculated risks and step outside your comfort zone.

Best days of the month: May 7th, 13th, 18th, 19th, 23rd, 28th and 29th.

June 2024

Horoscope

June brings a dynamic and transformative energy for Capricorn individuals. It is a month of growth, self-discovery, and new beginnings. The celestial configurations encourage you to step out of your comfort zone and embrace change.

This month, you may feel a strong urge to explore different aspects of your life, both internally and externally. The Mars-Uranus semi-sextile on June 1st ignites your desire for freedom and independence. It motivates you to break free from old patterns and embrace a more authentic expression of yourself.

The Sun's quintile with Neptune on June 1st enhances your intuition and spiritual connection. You may find inspiration in your dreams and inner visions, guiding you towards greater clarity and understanding.

Mercury's conjunction with Jupiter on June 4th amplifies your communication skills and intellectual pursuits. This alignment supports learning, networking, and expanding your knowledge base. It is a favorable time for educational pursuits, writing, or sharing your ideas with others.

The Sun's conjunction with Venus on June 4th brings harmony, love, and a greater appreciation for beauty into your life. This alignment enhances your relationships, both romantic and platonic, and encourages you to nurture and express your affections.

The Venus-Saturn square on June 8th may bring some challenges in your relationships or finances. It calls for a balance between responsibility and personal desires. Exercise caution in financial matters and maintain open and honest communication in your relationships.

The Mercury-Saturn square on June 12th may bring temporary obstacles in your communication and decision-making. It is important to stay patient, thorough, and diligent in your actions. Use this time to review and reassess your plans before moving forward.

The Sun's square with Neptune on June 20th cautions against illusion and confusion. Be mindful of deception or self-deception, and seek clarity and discernment in your interactions and decisions.

Overall, June presents a transformative and introspective period for Capricorn individuals. Embrace change, trust your intuition, and focus on personal growth and self-discovery.

Love

In June, Capricorn individuals experience significant developments in their love lives. The celestial aspects create a harmonious and passionate energy, fostering deeper connections and romantic encounters.

The Sun's conjunction with Venus on June 4th brings a wave of love, beauty, and harmony into your relationships. This alignment enhances your ability to express your affections and strengthens the bond with your partner. If single, this alignment increases your magnetism and attractiveness, making you more open to love and new connections.

The Venus-Mars sextile on June 11th sparks passion and desire in your romantic relationships. It ignites a sense of adventure and encourages you to explore new dimensions of intimacy and pleasure with your partner. It is an ideal time for rekindling the flames of passion or embarking on new romantic adventures.

The Venus-Neptune square on June 16th may introduce some illusions or idealizations in your love life. It is important to stay grounded and maintain realistic expectations. Communication and clarity are key to navigating any challenges that arise during this time.

The Sun's sextile with Chiron on June 22nd promotes healing and growth within your relationships. It offers an opportunity for deeper understanding, forgiveness, and emotional healing. Use this energy to address any lingering wounds or conflicts and foster a stronger and more compassionate connection with your partner.

The Mercury-Venus conjunction on June 17th enhances your communication skills and charm. It supports meaningful conversations, expressions of love, and the ability to truly listen and understand your partner's needs and desires.

Whether single or in a relationship, June encourages you to be open to new possibilities and experiences in love. Embrace the transformative energy and allow your heart to guide you towards deeper connections and fulfillment.

Career

The Mercury-Jupiter conjunction on June 4th amplifies your communication skills and intellectual prowess. It is a favorable time for networking, sharing your ideas, and expanding your professional connections. This alignment supports educational pursuits and may bring exciting opportunities for learning or teaching.

The Mars-Neptune semi-sextile on June 8th inspires creativity and intuition in your work. It encourages you to think outside the box and explore innovative solutions to challenges. Trust your instincts and tap into your imaginative abilities to make significant progress in your projects or career goals.

The Sun's square with Saturn on June 9th may present temporary obstacles or delays in your professional endeavors. It calls for discipline, patience, and perseverance. Stay focused on your long-term goals and maintain a practical approach to overcome any challenges that arise.

The Mercury-Saturn square on June 12th may bring some communication or decision-making challenges in your work environment. It is important to remain diligent, thorough, and detail-oriented in your tasks. Double-check your work and ensure clarity in your communication to avoid misunderstandings.

The Sun's square with Neptune on June 20th cautions against deception or confusion in your professional interactions. Be vigilant and maintain clear boundaries in your work relationships. Trust your instincts and seek clarity before making important decisions.

Finance

June brings a mix of financial opportunities and cautionary aspects for Capricorn individuals. It is a month to be mindful of your financial decisions and maintain a balanced approach to money matters.

The Venus-Saturn square on June 8th may introduce some financial challenges or restrictions. It calls for responsible financial management and prudent decision-making. Avoid impulsive purchases or risky investments during this time. Focus on long-term stability and exercise caution in your financial transactions.

The Venus-Neptune square on June 16th warns against illusions or deceptions in your financial dealings. Be cautious of potential scams or unrealistic promises. It is important to conduct thorough research and seek professional advice before making any major financial decisions.

The Mercury-Saturn square on June 12th may bring some financial constraints or delays. It is essential to exercise patience and budget your resources wisely. Review your financial plans and make necessary adjustments to ensure stability and avoid unnecessary expenses.

The Mercury-Jupiter conjunction on June 4th may bring positive financial opportunities through networking, education, or expanding your professional connections. It is a favorable time to seek financial advice or explore new income streams. Stay open to learning and strategic investments that align with your long-term goals.

The Sun's square with Saturn on June 9th reminds you to exercise discipline and responsibility in your financial matters. Stick to your budget and avoid impulsive spending. Delay major financial decisions until you have thoroughly evaluated all the risks and rewards.

Health

June places a strong focus on self-care and holistic well-being for Capricorn individuals. The celestial aspects encourage you to prioritize your health and establish sustainable routines for physical and mental well-being.

The Mars-Neptune semi-sextile on June 8th inspires you to explore alternative healing modalities and tap into your intuitive wisdom for optimal health. Listen to your body's signals and pay attention to any emotional or energetic imbalances that may be affecting your well-being. Incorporate mindfulness practices, meditation, or gentle exercises into your routine to restore harmony and balance.

The Sun's sextile with Chiron on June 22nd promotes emotional healing and self-acceptance. It encourages you to address any underlying emotional wounds or patterns that may be impacting your health. Seek support from trusted professionals or therapists if needed, as they can provide valuable guidance on your healing journey.

The Mercury-Venus conjunction on June 17th enhances your ability to communicate your needs and desires, both to yourself and to others. Use this alignment to express your emotions, establish healthy boundaries, and nurture positive relationships that contribute to your overall well-being.

The Sun's square with Neptune on June 20th calls for caution in terms of your physical and emotional boundaries. Be mindful of potential energy drains or situations that compromise your well-being. Prioritize self-care, rest, and rejuvenation to maintain optimal health during this time.

Travel

The Mars-Neptune semi-sextile on June 8th ignites your wanderlust and desire for adventure. It inspires you to explore new destinations or revisit familiar places with a fresh perspective. Trust your intuition and follow your heart's desires when planning your travels.

The Mercury-Jupiter conjunction on June 4th enhances your communication skills and intellectual curiosity. This alignment supports educational trips, cultural exchanges, or networking events. Consider combining your love for learning with your travel plans, as it can lead to enriching experiences and meaningful connections.

The Sun's square with Saturn on June 9th may introduce some delays or obstacles in your travel plans. It is essential to stay flexible and adaptable, as unexpected changes may arise. Maintain open communication with travel companions or organizers to navigate any challenges smoothly.

The Sun's square with Neptune on June 20th reminds you to stay vigilant during your travels. Be cautious of potential scams or deceptive situations. Research your destinations, take necessary safety precautions, and trust your instincts to ensure a safe and enjoyable travel experience.

Insight from the stars

The Mars-Neptune semi-sextile on June 8th infuses your life with an adventurous and imaginative spirit. It's a perfect time to indulge in creative hobbies, explore new recreational activities, or reconnect with your sense of fun.

Best days of the month: June 4th, 11th, 17th, 20th, 22nd, 26th, and 29th.

July 2024

Horoscope

The Jupiter-Chiron semi-square on July 1st may bring up some emotional wounds or limiting beliefs that need to be addressed. Use this energy to engage in self-healing and seek support from trusted individuals or therapists who can assist you in your journey of personal growth.

The Sun's square with Uranus on July 1st encourages you to embrace change and release old patterns that no longer serve your highest good. Be open to unexpected opportunities and be willing to step outside of your comfort zone to experience personal breakthroughs.

The Mercury-Neptune trine on July 2nd enhances your intuition and creative expression. It's a favorable time for introspection, journaling, or engaging in artistic pursuits that allow you to tap into your inner wisdom.

The Venus-Saturn trine on July 2nd provides stability and support in your relationships. It fosters commitment, loyalty, and mutual understanding. If you're in a partnership, this alignment encourages you to deepen your connection through open communication and shared responsibilities.

The Mars-Saturn sextile on July 5th empowers you to take practical and disciplined actions in your career and ambitions. It's a favorable time to work hard, stay focused, and persevere in achieving your professional goals.

The Sun's square with Chiron on July 15th may bring emotional challenges or triggers related to your self-worth and personal identity. Use this opportunity to engage in self-care practices, seek inner healing, and practice self-compassion.

The Jupiter-Neptune quintile on July 18th invites you to explore your spiritual or philosophical beliefs and tap into your intuition. It supports your quest for higher knowledge and understanding.

Love

The Venus-Saturn trine on July 2nd supports stable and committed partnerships. It encourages open communication, shared responsibilities, and a sense of security within your relationship. This alignment fosters loyalty, trust, and long-lasting love.

The Mars-Saturn sextile on July 5th emphasizes the importance of patience, dedication, and hard work in maintaining a harmonious relationship. Use this energy to address any unresolved conflicts, strengthen your emotional bond, and build a solid foundation for the future.

The Venus-Neptune trine on July 11th enhances your romantic and compassionate nature. It brings a sense of dreaminess and inspiration to your love life. This alignment encourages acts of kindness, emotional connection, and the expression of unconditional love towards your partner.

The Sun's square with Chiron on July 15th may bring up emotional wounds or insecurities in relationships. It's essential to practice self-compassion and open communication to navigate any challenges that arise. Seek support from your partner and cultivate a safe space for vulnerability and healing.

The Venus-Jupiter sextile on July 21st brings joy, positivity, and adventure to your love life. It's a favorable time for exploring new experiences, going on romantic getaways, or engaging in activities that reignite the spark in your relationship.

The Venus-Chiron trine on July 30th invites you to embrace vulnerability and emotional healing within your relationship. It encourages open-hearted conversations and the expression of empathy and compassion towards your partner.

Career

The Mars-Saturn sextile on July 5th empowers you to take practical and disciplined actions towards your career aspirations. It's a favorable time to work hard, stay focused, and demonstrate your reliability and dedication to your superiors and colleagues.

The Sun's square with Chiron on July 15th may bring up insecurities or emotional wounds related to your professional identity. It's crucial to engage in self-reflection and address any limiting beliefs that may hinder your growth. Use this opportunity to practice self-compassion and redefine your sense of worth and purpose in your career.

The Venus-Saturn trine on July 2nd supports stability and commitment in your work environment. It encourages collaboration, open communication, and a sense of loyalty and mutual support among colleagues. This alignment is favorable for long-term projects and building strong professional relationships.

The Jupiter-Neptune quintile on July 18th invites you to tap into your intuition and explore innovative approaches to your work. It's a favorable time to trust your instincts and think outside the box. Embrace your creative side and allow your imagination to guide you towards new opportunities and solutions.

The Mercury-Jupiter sextile on July 19th enhances your communication skills and expands your knowledge base. It's a favorable time to engage in networking, seek mentorship, or pursue further education or training that can enhance your career prospects.

The Mercury-Saturn biquintile on July 30th empowers you with practical problem-solving skills and attention to detail. Use this energy to tackle challenging tasks, implement efficient systems, and demonstrate your reliability and competence to superiors.

Finance

The Venus-Saturn trine on July 2nd supports financial stability and disciplined money management. It encourages you to make responsible choices, budget wisely, and establish a solid foundation for your financial future. This alignment emphasizes the importance of long-term investments and savings.

The Sun's square with Chiron on July 15th may bring up financial insecurities or wounds related to self-worth. Use this opportunity to address any limiting beliefs around money and reframe your mindset to one of abundance and financial empowerment. Seek professional advice if needed to improve your financial literacy and make informed decisions.

The Mars-Saturn sextile on July 5th urges you to be diligent and disciplined in your financial endeavors. It's a favorable time to work towards financial goals, pay off debts, and establish a sense of financial security. Take practical steps towards achieving financial independence and consider long-term strategies.

The Jupiter-Neptune quintile on July 18th invites you to trust your intuition in financial matters. Listen to your inner guidance when making financial decisions and be open to unconventional opportunities. However, exercise caution and do thorough research before committing to any financial ventures.

The Venus-Neptune trine on July 11th enhances your ability to attract financial abundance through creative endeavors or compassionate acts. It's a favorable time to explore side hustles or pursue projects that align with your passions and can generate additional income.

The Mercury-Saturn biquintile on July 30th supports practical financial planning and attention to detail. Use this energy to review your financial goals, create a realistic budget, and consider long-term investments that align with your values and financial aspirations.

Health

The Sun's square with Chiron on July 15th may bring up emotional wounds or vulnerabilities that can impact your overall well-being. It's crucial to practice self-compassion, engage in stress-management techniques, and seek support if needed. Focus on activities that nurture your emotional health, such as journaling, meditation, or therapy.

The Mars-Saturn sextile on July 5th empowers you with discipline and determination to pursue a healthy lifestyle. It's a favorable time to establish or reinforce healthy habits, such as regular exercise, balanced nutrition, and sufficient rest. Set achievable fitness goals and stay committed to them.

The Venus-Neptune trine on July 11th encourages self-care practices that promote emotional and mental well-being. Engage in activities that bring you joy and relaxation, such as spending time in nature, practicing mindfulness, or indulging in creative outlets.

The Mercury-Saturn biquintile on July 30th supports practical self-care routines and attention to detail in your health regimen. Take time to assess your physical needs, schedule regular check-ups, and ensure you are maintaining a balanced lifestyle.

The Jupiter-Neptune quintile on July 18th invites you to explore holistic approaches to your health. Consider alternative therapies, such as acupuncture or energy healing, to support your overall well-being. Trust your intuition when making health-related decisions and seek guidance from professionals if necessary.

The Venus-Saturn trine on July 2nd emphasizes the importance of self-love and self-care in maintaining overall health. Prioritize activities that nourish your soul and bring you a sense of fulfillment and contentment. Take time for yourself and establish healthy boundaries to prevent burnout.

Travel

The Mars-Uranus conjunction on July 15th sparks a sense of spontaneity and a desire for unique travel experiences. Consider exploring off-the-beaten-path destinations or engaging in activities that push you outside of your comfort zone. Embrace the unexpected and allow yourself to be open to new adventures.

The Sun's square with Jupiter on July 23rd may bring challenges or delays in travel plans. It's important to remain flexible and adaptable during this time. Use this opportunity to practice patience and find alternative ways to satisfy your wanderlust, such as exploring local attractions or planning future trips.

The Venus-Uranus trine on July 8th enhances the potential for unexpected encounters and serendipitous experiences during your travels. Embrace spontaneity and be open to new connections or opportunities that may arise.

The Mercury-Uranus square on July 21st encourages you to be mindful of communication and logistics during your travels. Double-check travel arrangements, stay organized, and be prepared for possible delays or changes. It's a favorable time to embrace technology and utilize travel apps or tools to enhance your travel experience.

The Jupiter-Neptune quintile on July 18th invites you to approach your travels with a sense of wonder and curiosity. Embrace the spirit of adventure and seek out experiences that align with your personal interests and values. Engage with the local culture, try new cuisines, and immerse yourself in the unique aspects of the destinations you visit.

The Sun's opposition with Pluto on July 23rd may bring power struggles or control issues during your travels. It's essential to maintain a balanced perspective, practice assertiveness, and establish healthy boundaries when encountering challenging situations. Prioritize your safety and well-being while enjoying your travel experiences.

Insight from the stars

his is the month to break free from routine, let loose, and create stories that will be the talk of the town. Enjoy the ride, Capricorn, and make July a month to remember!

Best days of the month: July 8th, 11th, 18th, 23rd, 26th, 30th, and 31st.

August 2024

Horoscope

Dear Capricorn, get ready for an eventful and transformative month ahead in August! The planetary aspects will have a significant impact on various areas of your life, offering both opportunities and challenges for personal growth and evolution.

With Mars in Gemini sextile True Node in Aries, your communication skills will be heightened, and networking opportunities will arise. This is a favorable time for expressing your ideas, negotiating deals, and collaborating with others. Use your persuasive abilities and assertiveness to make progress in your professional and personal relationships.

Venus in Leo will ignite your romantic side and boost your creative energy. As Venus squares Uranus in Taurus, unexpected romantic encounters or exciting social events may come your way. Embrace the spontaneity and allow yourself to experience the thrill of new connections and adventures. Your artistic talents will flourish during this time, so channel your creativity into projects that bring you joy and satisfaction.

However, be prepared for some challenging aspects as the Sun quincunxes Saturn in Pisces and sesquiquadrates Chiron in Aries. You may experience a conflict between your ambitions and your emotional well-being. It's essential to find a balance between your career aspirations and taking care of your mental and emotional health. Focus on establishing healthy boundaries and practicing self-care to maintain a sense of stability and inner peace.

August also presents an opportunity for introspection and healing, as Mercury trines Chiron. Take this time to reflect on past wounds and engage in self-reflection. Consider seeking support from a therapist or engaging in spiritual practices to facilitate emotional healing and personal growth.

Love

In matters of the heart, Capricorn, August brings a mix of excitement and unpredictability. With Venus in Leo square Uranus in Taurus, expect unexpected twists and turns in your love life. Sudden attractions or surprises may shake up your existing relationships or bring new people into your life. Embrace the spontaneity and be open to exploring new connections.

For those in committed relationships, the square between Venus and Uranus may create some tension or a desire for freedom. It's important to maintain open and honest communication with your partner to navigate any challenges that arise. Find creative ways to inject passion and excitement into your relationship while respecting each other's need for independence.

If you're single, this is an excellent time to venture outside your comfort zone and try new dating experiences. Social events, parties, or group activities can lead to exciting encounters. However, remember to listen to your intuition and take things at a pace that feels right for you.

Career

August presents several opportunities for career growth and advancement for Capricorn. With Mars in Gemini sextile True Node in Aries, your communication skills and networking abilities will play a vital role in your professional success. Focus on building connections, sharing your ideas, and collaborating with others.

This month, you may find yourself involved in negotiations or deal-making, as Venus in Leo squares Uranus in Taurus. Trust your instincts and be open to innovative solutions. However, exercise caution in making impulsive decisions and ensure you thoroughly evaluate any agreements or contracts before finalizing them.

Capricorn, your natural ambition and hard work will be recognized as the Sun quincunxes Saturn in Pisces. Your dedication and commitment to your goals will not go unnoticed. This aspect encourages you to persevere through challenges and demonstrate your leadership skills.

Stay adaptable and open to learning opportunities, as Mercury trines Chiron. Engage in professional development, seek out mentors, or attend workshops that expand your skillset and enhance your career prospects. Remember to maintain a healthy work-life balance and prioritize self-care to avoid burnout.

Finance

Capricorn, your financial outlook in August is influenced by the square between Venus in Leo and Uranus in Taurus. This aspect may bring unexpected expenses or financial fluctuations. It's crucial to exercise caution and maintain a balanced approach to money matters.

Avoid impulsive spending and focus on budgeting and saving. Review your financial goals and consider seeking advice from a financial planner or advisor to make informed decisions. Look for innovative ways to increase your income or explore new investment opportunities.

The Sun's quincunx aspect with Saturn reminds you to maintain discipline and be cautious with financial commitments. Take a conservative approach to long-term investments and assess risks carefully. Avoid making hasty decisions and rely on thorough research and expert guidance before entering into any significant financial agreements.

.

Health

Capricorn, your well-being in August requires attention and self-care. The Sun's quincunx aspect with Saturn reminds you to find a balance between your professional responsibilities and your physical and mental health. Avoid overextending yourself and prioritize self-care practices.

With Mars in Gemini sextile True Node in Aries, physical exercise and active pursuits will benefit you greatly. Engage in activities that get you moving, such as jogging, dancing, or participating in team sports. This will not only boost your physical fitness but also enhance your mood and overall well-being.

The trine between Mercury and Chiron encourages you to focus on emotional healing and self-reflection. Take time for introspection, engage in mindfulness practices, and seek support from therapists or healers if needed. Journaling or engaging in creative outlets can also help you process emotions and maintain mental equilibrium.

Maintain a balanced diet and prioritize nutritious meals. Consider exploring new recipes or incorporating superfoods into your diet to boost your energy levels. Adequate rest and relaxation are essential, so ensure you are getting enough quality sleep each night.

If you find yourself feeling overwhelmed or stressed, don't hesitate to seek support from loved ones or professionals. Prioritizing your well-being will enable you to navigate the demands of daily life with resilience and vitality.

Travel

With Mars in Gemini sextile True Node in Aries, this is an ideal time to plan short trips or weekend getaways. Embrace the adventurous spirit and seek out new experiences that broaden your horizons.

As Venus squares Uranus, unexpected travel opportunities may arise. Be open to spontaneous adventures or invitations to travel. However, maintain flexibility in your plans, as there may be unexpected changes or delays along the way.

When traveling, ensure you take necessary precautions and prioritize safety. Pay attention to travel advisories, follow health guidelines, and make informed decisions about your destinations.

Travel can provide a refreshing break from routine and offer opportunities for personal growth. Embrace the diversity of new cultures, try local cuisines, and engage in immersive experiences. Whether you're exploring new cities or reconnecting with nature, allow yourself to be fully present and open to the transformative power of travel.

Insight from the stars

Embrace the joy of the present moment and cultivate a playful spirit. Remember, life is an adventure, and sometimes the craziest fun comes from unexpected experiences.

Best days of the month: August 1st, 10th, 15th, 22nd, 25th, 27th and 30th.

September 2024

Horoscope

The month begins with Mercury trine Chiron, allowing you to communicate your emotions and heal any past wounds. This aspect encourages you to express your vulnerability and seek understanding from those around you.

With the Sun quintile Mars, you will feel a surge of motivation and assertiveness. This energy empowers you to take charge of your life and pursue your goals with determination. Use this period to make bold decisions and assert your boundaries.

However, the square between Mars and Neptune on September 3rd cautions against impulsive actions or unrealistic expectations. Remain grounded and seek clarity before committing to any major endeavors. Trust your intuition and discern between genuine opportunities and illusory distractions.

In love and relationships, Venus opposes the True Node, creating a dynamic tension between commitment and independence. This aspect urges you to find a balance between your personal needs and the expectations of your partner. Embrace open communication and compromise to navigate any relationship challenges.

Love

The opposition between Venus and the True Node emphasizes the need for balance and compromise in relationships. It's important to honor your own desires while considering the needs and aspirations of your partner.

For those in committed relationships, this aspect may bring a deeper understanding of each other's desires and goals. Use this time to reevaluate your shared visions and make adjustments to strengthen the bond between you. Cultivate open and honest communication, allowing for growth and mutual support.

If you're single, this aspect can lead to fated encounters or unexpected attractions. Stay open to new connections and embrace the possibilities that come your way. However, avoid rushing into commitments and take time to evaluate the long-term compatibility of potential partners.

Emotional vulnerability and self-reflection are essential during this period. Seek clarity within yourself before pursuing a new romance, ensuring that your choices align with your values and aspirations. Trust your intuition to guide you towards relationships that support your personal growth and happiness.

Career

With Mars trine Saturn, your determination and discipline will lead to tangible results. Take advantage of this supportive energy by setting clear goals and implementing structured plans.

The Sun's opposition to Saturn reminds you to find a balance between ambition and self-care. While it's important to dedicate yourself to your career, remember to prioritize your well-being and maintain a healthy work-life balance. Avoid overextending yourself and recognize the importance of rest and rejuvenation.

Mercury's opposition to the True Node indicates the need for effective communication and collaboration in the workplace. Embrace teamwork and seek out opportunities for networking and forming alliances. Your ability to connect with others and share your ideas will greatly contribute to your professional success.

Capricorn, this is also a period to refine your skills and enhance your expertise. Engage in professional development and seek out mentors or courses that expand your knowledge. Embrace new technologies and stay up to date with industry trends to remain competitive in your field.

Finance

The Sun's opposition to Neptune cautions against financial illusions and unrealistic expectations. Avoid impulsive spending or risky investments during this period.

Focus on budgeting and reviewing your financial goals. Seek professional advice if needed and take a practical and disciplined approach to managing your money. Consider long-term financial stability and make informed decisions based on thorough research and analysis.

The trine between Venus and Jupiter offers some positive financial opportunities. This aspect brings luck and abundance, but it's important to exercise caution and not rely solely on chance. Combine your hard work and dedication with a mindful approach to finances to make the most of this favorable energy.

Capricorn, prioritize saving and building a solid financial foundation. Consider long-term investments or retirement planning to ensure your financial security. Avoid unnecessary risks and stay focused on your financial goals.

107

Health

A The opposition between the Sun and Neptune may affect your energy levels and overall well-being. Be mindful of stress and take proactive measures to manage it effectively.

Engage in stress-relief activities such as yoga, meditation, or regular exercise. These practices will not only help you manage stress but also improve your overall physical and mental well-being. Prioritize quality sleep and establish a consistent sleep routine.

Nurture your body with nutritious meals and a balanced diet. Incorporate fresh fruits, vegetables, and whole grains into your meals, providing your body with essential nutrients. Stay hydrated and limit the consumption of processed foods and sugary beverages.

Maintain a regular exercise routine that suits your preferences and lifestyle. Find activities that you enjoy, such as walking, jogging, or joining a fitness class. Physical activity will boost your energy levels, improve mood, and promote overall health.

Take time for self-reflection and emotional well-being. Engage in activities that bring you joy and relaxation, such as hobbies, creative pursuits, or spending time in nature. Prioritize your mental health and seek support from therapists or counselors if needed.

Stay mindful of your emotional state and practice self-compassion. Be gentle with yourself during challenging times and allow space for emotional processing. Surround yourself with a supportive network of loved ones who uplift and encourage you.

Travel

With Mars square the True Node, there may be a desire for adventure and new experiences. Embrace the spirit of spontaneity and be open to unexpected travel opportunities that arise.

When planning your travels, consider destinations that offer a mix of relaxation and adventure. Seek out places that provide opportunities for both rejuvenation and exploration. Whether it's a beach getaway or an adventurous hiking trip, find a balance that suits your preferences.

When traveling, stay adaptable and be prepared for potential changes or delays. Keep track of travel advisories and follow health guidelines to ensure a safe and enjoyable trip. Plan ahead and make necessary arrangements to make your journey smoother.

Immerse yourself in the local culture and embrace the diversity of new experiences. Engage with the locals, try traditional cuisine, and visit historical or natural landmarks. Travel can be a transformative experience that broadens your perspectives and fosters personal growth.

Capricorn, remember to find moments of solitude and reflection during your travels. Take time to recharge and connect with yourself amidst the excitement of new environments. Journaling or capturing memories through photography can be a meaningful way to document your experiences.

Insight from the stars

Capricorn, the stars encourage you to embrace your creative side. Engage in artistic pursuits, try new hobbies, and let your imagination run wild.

Best days of the month: September 2nd, 10th, 12th, 15th, 19th 26th and 30th.

October 2024

Horoscope

Embrace the transformative energy that permeates this month and use it to shed old patterns and beliefs that no longer serve you. Focus on personal growth and self-improvement. Dive into your emotions and embrace vulnerability, as this will lead to profound healing and personal development.

Relationships and connections play a significant role this month. The alignment between Venus and the True Node on October 3 encourages meaningful encounters and deep connections. Whether in friendships or romantic relationships, prioritize authenticity and open communication. Nurture your connections and foster mutual support and understanding.

Stay attuned to the balance between your personal needs and the needs of your relationships. Avoid becoming overly self-focused or neglecting your loved ones. Find harmony in balancing your own growth with maintaining strong and healthy connections.

Love

Capricorn, October brings a deepening of emotional connections in your love life. The alignment between Venus and Neptune on October 15 enhances romantic experiences and fosters a sense of spiritual and emotional connection with your partner. This is a time to embrace romance, express your affection, and deepen the bond with your loved one.

For those who are single, this month offers opportunities for meaningful connections. The alignment between Venus and Jupiter on October 23 brings a sense of optimism and expansion in your social life. Open yourself to new possibilities and be receptive to meeting someone special.

However, it's important to maintain a balance between your personal growth and your relationships. The alignment between Venus and Saturn on October 28 reminds you to prioritize stability and commitment in your love life. Ensure that your actions align with your long-term relationship goals and that you invest time and effort into building a solid foundation.

Communication and open dialogue are key to fostering healthy relationships. Use the energy of Mercury's opposition to Uranus on October 30 to express your thoughts and emotions with clarity and authenticity. This alignment encourages honest conversations that can lead to growth and understanding in your relationships.

Career

In October, Capricorn, your career takes center stage. The alignment between Mercury and Mars on October 6 enhances your assertiveness and communication skills, making it a favorable time to present your ideas, negotiate contracts, or showcase your professional abilities.

This month, you may feel driven to take on new challenges and expand your skill set. The alignment between Mercury and Jupiter on October 8 supports your intellectual growth and encourages you to pursue learning opportunities or engage in professional development. Embrace these opportunities to enhance your career prospects.

Capricorn, the alignment between the Sun and Pluto on October 22 empowers you to tap into your personal power and make strategic career moves. Use this energy to set clear goals, develop a solid plan of action, and take calculated risks. Trust your instincts and rely on your determination and hard work to achieve success.

It's crucial to maintain a healthy work-life balance. The alignment between Venus and Mars on October 8 reminds you to find harmony between your professional aspirations and your personal relationships. Prioritize self-care and nurture your well-being to sustain your productivity and overall satisfaction in your career.

Finance

Capricorn, October brings opportunities for financial stability and growth. The alignment between Venus and Saturn on October 4 emphasizes the importance of financial responsibility and discipline. This is a favorable time to reevaluate your budget, assess your long-term financial goals, and make necessary adjustments.

The alignment between Venus and Jupiter on October 5 opens doors for financial expansion and abundance. Be open to new income streams and seize opportunities for growth. However, exercise caution and avoid impulsive spending or risky investments. It's essential to strike a balance between enjoying the fruits of your labor and maintaining a secure financial foundation.

This month, focus on long-term financial planning and investment strategies. The alignment between Mercury and Neptune on October 16 enhances your intuitive abilities and helps you make sound financial decisions. Trust your instincts and seek expert advice when needed.

114

Capricorn, the alignment between Venus and Pluto on October 17 encourages you to take control of your financial situation and transform any limiting beliefs or patterns around money. This is a time to embrace financial empowerment and create a solid financial future.

Remember to prioritize financial well-being alongside your other goals. The alignment between Mercury and Chiron on October 27 reminds you to nurture your relationship with money and address any emotional blocks or beliefs that may hinder your financial growth. Cultivate a positive mindset and abundance mentality to attract prosperity into your life.

Health

In October, Capricorn, prioritize your physical and mental well-being. The alignment between the Sun and Uranus on October 4 brings a burst of vitality and energy. Use this renewed vigor to establish healthy habits and commit to regular exercise routines. Engage in activities that bring you joy and help you maintain an active lifestyle.

Self-care and stress management are crucial for your overall health. The alignment between Venus and Saturn on October 4 reminds you to establish healthy boundaries and find balance between your personal and professional life. Take time to relax, recharge, and engage in activities that promote inner peace and relaxation.

Capricorn, the alignment between Mercury and Neptune on October 12 encourages you to prioritize mental and emotional well-being. Practice mindfulness, meditation, or journaling to calm your mind and gain clarity. Seek emotional support when needed and don't hesitate to reach out to a trusted therapist or counselor.

It's essential to maintain a healthy diet and prioritize nutritious meals. The alignment between Venus and Mars on October 8 supports your efforts to nourish your body with wholesome foods. Focus on incorporating fresh fruits, vegetables, and whole grains into your diet. Stay hydrated and ensure you're getting enough restful sleep to support your overall health.

Travel

The alignment between Mercury and Jupiter on October 8 enhances your curiosity and desire to explore new horizons. Consider planning a trip to a destination that sparks your interest or immersing yourself in a different culture.

If travel plans are not feasible this month, you can still satisfy your wanderlust by engaging in local adventures or planning day trips to nearby attractions.

Discover hidden gems in your own backyard and embrace the spirit of exploration.

The alignment between Venus and Mars on October 8 encourages romantic getaways or travel experiences with your loved one. Whether it's a weekend escape or a longer vacation, prioritize quality time together and create lasting memories.

When traveling, ensure you prioritize your well-being and safety. Stay organized, double-check travel arrangements, and adhere to any necessary health and safety guidelines. Take time to relax and savor the moments of relaxation and rejuvenation that travel brings.

Capricorn, use travel as an opportunity for personal growth and self-discovery. Allow yourself to step out of your comfort zone and embrace new experiences. Whether it's trying local cuisines, engaging in adventure activities, or connecting with locals, let the spirit of travel expand your horizons and bring joy to your life.

Insight from the stars

Capricorn, embrace the unexpected and let your wild side shine. Take a spontaneous dance class, sing your heart out at karaoke, or indulge in a creative hobby.

Best days of the month: October 4th, 8th, 15th, 17th, 22nd, 27th and 31st

November 2024

Horoscope

The alignment between Jupiter and Chiron on November 2 encourages healing and self-discovery. Embrace personal growth and explore your beliefs and philosophies. This is a time for expanding your horizons and gaining a deeper understanding of yourself and the world around you.

Relationships take center stage this month, Capricorn. The alignment between Venus and Jupiter on November 3 sparks romantic and social connections. Open your heart to new experiences and deepen existing bonds. The alignment between the Sun and Saturn on November 4 highlights the importance of commitment and stability in your relationships. Focus on nurturing and strengthening the connections that matter to you.

Love

In matters of the heart, Capricorn, November brings significant opportunities for deepening emotional connections and fostering harmonious relationships. The alignment between Venus and Jupiter on November 3 enhances your natural charm and charisma, making you irresistible to others. This is a time for romance, socializing, and expanding your circle of friends.

If you're in a committed relationship, the alignment between Venus and Mars on November 7 ignites passion and intensifies the emotional bond with your partner. It's a favorable time for intimate moments and rekindling the spark in your relationship. Express your love and affection openly and make an effort to create meaningful experiences together.

For single Capricorns, the alignment between Venus and Uranus on November 12 brings unexpected and exciting encounters. Be open to new connections and embrace spontaneity in your love life. Trust your instincts and follow your heart, as this may lead you to a transformative romantic experience.

Communication is key in relationships, Capricorn. The alignment between Mercury and Jupiter on November 18 enhances your ability to express your feelings and articulate your needs. Take time to engage in heartfelt conversations with your partner and deepen your emotional connection.

Career

The alignment between Mercury and Mars on November 2 boosts your mental agility and assertiveness in the workplace. This is a favorable time for negotiations, presenting ideas, and taking the lead on projects.

The alignment between Venus and Saturn on November 22 encourages you to focus on long-term career goals and establish a solid foundation. Take calculated risks and demonstrate your reliability and dedication to your work. Your disciplined approach and attention to detail will be noticed by superiors and colleagues.

This month, it's crucial to balance ambition with self-care. The alignment between Mercury and Venus on November 26 reminds you to prioritize your well-being while pursuing your career goals. Take breaks when needed, engage in self-reflection, and find moments of peace amidst your busy schedule.

Capricorn, the alignment between Jupiter and the True Node on November 29 brings transformative energy to your career path. Trust the process and remain open to new opportunities and possibilities.

Embrace growth and expand your professional network. Seek guidance from mentors and tap into your inner wisdom to make informed career decisions.

Finance

Capricorn, November presents a mixed financial outlook. The alignment between Mercury and Mars on November 2 enhances your financial acumen and encourages proactive financial planning. This is a favorable time to analyze your expenses, create a budget, and explore new investment opportunities.

However, the alignment between Venus and Neptune on November 9 urges caution when it comes to financial decisions. Beware of impulsive spending or risky investments. Take time to evaluate potential risks and seek expert advice when needed.

The alignment between Venus and Jupiter on November 16 brings opportunities for financial growth and abundance. Stay open to new income streams and embrace positive money mindset. Focus on long-term financial planning and prioritize saving for the future.

Capricorn, the alignment between Venus and Chiron on November 27 reminds you to heal any emotional wounds or limiting beliefs around money. Practice gratitude and abundance mindset to attract financial prosperity into your life. Seek support from financial advisors or mentors to gain a clearer understanding of your financial goals and strategies.

Health

Capricorn, your well-being should be a top priority in November. The alignment between Mercury and Mars on November 2 boosts your physical energy and mental focus. Use this heightened vitality to engage in regular exercise, maintain a balanced diet, and prioritize self-care practices.

However, the alignment between the Sun and Neptune on November 4 reminds you to find a balance between productivity and rest. Avoid overworking yourself and listen to your body's signals for rest and rejuvenation. Incorporate relaxation techniques, such as meditation or yoga, into your daily routine to reduce stress and enhance overall well-being.

Capricorn, emotional well-being is equally important. The alignment between Venus and Saturn on November 12 encourages self-reflection and emotional healing. Take time for introspection, connect with your emotions, and seek support from trusted friends or professionals when needed.

The alignment between Venus and Uranus on November 14 brings opportunities for rejuvenation and trying new wellness practices. Explore alternative therapies or engage in creative outlets to express and release emotions.

Remember to prioritize self-care and maintain a healthy work-life balance. The alignment between the Sun and Mars on November 27 reminds you to assert healthy boundaries and avoid excessive stress. Make time for activities that bring you joy and relaxation, such as spending time in nature or engaging in hobbies.

Travel

Capricorn, November brings favorable energies for travel and exploration. The alignment between Mercury and Venus on November 7 enhances your communication skills, making it a great time for business trips or networking events. Embrace new cultural experiences and be open to forming meaningful connections with people from different backgrounds.

If you're considering a vacation, the alignment between Venus and Mars on November 8 brings opportunities for adventurous travel. Explore destinations that offer a balance of relaxation and exciting activities. Whether you're drawn to the serene beauty of nature or the vibrant energy of bustling cities, allow yourself to immerse in new environments and create lasting memories.

If travel is not feasible, consider local day trips or weekend getaways. Discover hidden gems in your own region and find joy in exploring nearby attractions. Remember that travel can also be an inner journey of self-discovery and growth. Take time for introspection and reflection, even if you're not physically traveling.

Capricorn, embrace the spirit of adventure and seize opportunities to broaden your horizons. The alignment between Mercury and Jupiter on November 29 encourages you to expand your knowledge and engage in intellectual pursuits. Consider attending workshops, conferences, or enrolling in courses that align with your interests.

Insight from the stars

"Embrace the unknown, for within it lie the seeds of growth and transformation. Trust in the journey, for the stars have aligned to guide you towards your highest potential. Have faith in your abilities, for you are capable of achieving greatness. Remember that true wisdom comes from both success and failure, so embrace every experience as a valuable lesson. Find joy in the present moment, for it is the only moment that truly exists. May your path be illuminated by the stars, and may you find fulfillment and purpose in every step you take."

Best days of the month: `November 2nd, 7th, 12th, 18th, 22nd, 26th and 29th.

December 2024

Horoscope

December brings a potent mix of cosmic energies that will have a profound impact on Capricorn. As the month begins, the Sun is in fiery Sagittarius, illuminating your sector of inner growth and spirituality. This alignment encourages you to delve deep within yourself, seeking wisdom and introspection. You may find yourself drawn to spiritual practices, meditation, or self-reflection to gain clarity and connect with your higher purpose.

Midway through the month, the Sun moves into your own sign of Capricorn, marking the beginning of your personal astrological year. This brings a surge of energy and vitality, invigorating your ambitions and aspirations. You'll feel a renewed sense of purpose and determination, ready to take on new challenges and achieve your goals. It's essential to harness this energy effectively and strike a balance between ambition and patience.

However, Saturn, your ruling planet, forms a square with Jupiter on December 24, which can create tension between your desire for expansion and your need for structure. You may feel a pull between exploring new horizons and adhering to established routines. The key is to find a middle ground that allows for growth while maintaining stability. Trust your inner wisdom to guide you in making the right decisions.

Love

In matters of the heart, December brings a transformative and passionate energy for Capricorn. Venus, the planet of love, enters your sign on December 4, intensifying your magnetism and enhancing your romantic appeal. This alignment empowers you to express your desires and attract positive connections. If you're single, this is an excellent time to put yourself out there and embrace new romantic opportunities. For those already in relationships, Venus's influence deepens your emotional bond and strengthens the connection with your partner.

On December 13, Venus forms a sextile with Chiron, the wounded healer, bringing an opportunity for healing and growth within your relationships. Use this energy to address any unresolved issues and foster greater understanding and compassion with your partner. Emotional vulnerability can lead to profound healing and transformation.

However, Venus's square with Uranus on December 28 may introduce some unpredictability or restlessness in your love life. Sudden changes or unexpected events could disrupt the harmony. It's crucial to remain open and adaptable during this time. Effective communication and a willingness to compromise will help navigate any challenges that arise. Embrace the transformative power of love and allow it to inspire personal growth within your relationships.

Career

The Sun's square with Saturn on December 4 may bring some obstacles or delays in your professional endeavors. This aspect tests your perseverance and commitment to your goals. Stay focused, determined, and patient during this time. Avoid succumbing to self-doubt or giving in to frustrations. Instead, use this period to refine your strategies, improve your skills, and prove your dedication.

The Sun's conjunction with Mercury on December 5 enhances your communication skills and intellectual abilities. This alignment favors collaborative projects, brainstorming sessions, and presenting your ideas with confidence. Your colleagues and superiors will recognize your contributions and value your input. Utilize this time to network, share your expertise, and make a lasting impression in your professional sphere.

Additionally, Mars, the planet of action and drive, forms a quintile with Uranus throughout December, stimulating innovation and creativity in your career. Embrace unconventional approaches, take calculated risks, and explore new ideas. This dynamic energy fuels your ambition and propels you towards success. Trust your instincts and seize opportunities that come your way. Your ability to adapt to changing circumstances will prove beneficial as you navigate the ever-evolving professional landscape.

Finance

Finances require careful consideration and planning in December, Capricorn. Venus's entry into your sign on December 4 blesses your financial sector with stability and abundance. You have the potential to attract prosperity and cultivate a secure financial foundation. This is an excellent time to evaluate your spending habits, create a budget, and focus on long-term financial goals.

The alignment between Venus and Uranus on December 2 brings the possibility of unexpected financial gains or innovative money-making opportunities. Stay open to new ventures and be willing to take calculated risks. However, Venus's square with Uranus on December 28 may introduce some instability or impulsive spending tendencies. Exercise caution and think before making major financial decisions. It's important to maintain a balanced approach and prioritize stability over short-term indulgences.

Consider seeking professional advice or engaging in financial planning to ensure a secure future. Wise investments and a disciplined approach to money management will serve you well. Utilize your practical nature and strategic thinking to make informed choices and maximize your financial potential. With diligent efforts and a long-term perspective, you can build a solid financial framework that supports your aspirations and provides a sense of security.

Health

December highlights the importance of holistic well-being for Capricorn. As the Sun transits through Sagittarius and Capricorn, pay attention to your physical, mental, and emotional health. The Sun's opposition to Jupiter on December 7 reminds you to strike a balance and avoid excesses in your daily routine. Overindulgence or neglecting self-care practices can lead to imbalances and low energy levels. Find a middle ground that nourishes your body and mind without compromising your overall well-being.

The Sun's trine with Chiron on December 10 supports healing and self-improvement. This aspect empowers you to address any lingering health concerns and adopt holistic approaches to wellness. Consider incorporating meditation, mindfulness practices, and gentle physical activities into your daily routine. Take time for self-reflection, identify areas of growth, and commit to positive lifestyle changes.

Prioritize adequate rest and quality sleep to replenish your energy levels. With the busy holiday season, make self-care a non-negotiable part of your routine. Delegate responsibilities when necessary, set boundaries, and practice saying no to avoid unnecessary stress and overwhelm.

Pay attention to your emotional well-being as well. Seek support from loved ones or consider therapy or counseling if needed. Emotional balance is key to overall health and vitality. Maintain a positive outlook, practice gratitude, and cultivate self-compassion.

Travel

December invites Capricorn to embrace adventure and expand horizons through travel. The Sun's alignment with Mars on December 20 ignites your wanderlust and ignites a desire for new experiences. Whether it's a spontaneous weekend getaway or a carefully planned international trip, seize the opportunity to explore unfamiliar territories and broaden your perspectives.

However, Mercury's square with Neptune on December 28 urges caution and attention to travel-related miscommunications or delays. Double-check travel itineraries, stay flexible in case of unexpected changes, and maintain open communication with travel companions. Embrace the spirit of adventure and be open to transformative experiences that travel can offer.

When planning your travels, consider destinations that offer a mix of relaxation and cultural immersion. Whether it's exploring historical sites, connecting with nature, or indulging in local cuisines, prioritize experiences that align with your interests and values. Traveling with loved ones or close friends can enhance the enjoyment and create lasting memories.

As you embark on your journeys, remember to take care of your well-being. Stay hydrated, get enough rest, and practice self-care even when away from home.

Engage in activities that rejuvenate and nourish your body and soul. Embrace the freedom and expansion that travel brings, and allow it to inspire personal growth and self-discovery.

Insight from the stars

"Balance ambition with patience and allow your intuition to guide your actions."

Best days of the month: `December 2nd, 10th, 15th, 19th, 20th, 24th, and 31st.

Printed in Great Britain
by Amazon

36483804R00077